Pygmalion

and Related Readings

McDougal Littell
A HOUGHTON MIFFLIN COMPANY

Evanston, Illinois   *Boston*   *Dallas*

Acknowledgments

Indiana University Press: Excerpt from *Metamorphoses* by Ovid, translated by Rolfe Humphries; Copyright 1955 by the Indiana University Press. Reprinted by permission of Indiana University Press.

Warner Bros. Publications Inc.: Excerpt from *My Fair Lady* by Alan Jay Lerner and Frederick Loewe; Copyright 1956 by Alan Jay Lerner (ASCAP) and Frederick Loewe (ASCAP). All rights administered by Chappell & Co. (ASCAP). All rights reserved. Reprinted by permission of Warner Bros. Publications U.S. Inc., Miami, FL 33014.

Peters, Fraser & Dunlop, and Faber and Faber Limited: Excerpt from "The London Language" from *The Story of English* by Robert McCrum, Robert MacNeil, and William Cran; Copyright © 1986 by Robert McCrum, Robert MacNeil, and William Cran. Reprinted by permission of Peters, Fraser & Dunlop and by permission of Faber and Faber Limited.

Sandra Dijkstra Literary Agency: "Mother Tongue" from *The Threepenny Review* by Amy Tan; Copyright © 1990 by Amy Tan. Reprinted by permission of the author and the Sandra Dijkstra Literary Agency.

Continued on page 214.

Cover illustration by Mark Braught.
Author photo: Hulton Deutsch.

ISBN 0-395-77555-8

9 10 11 12 13 14 15 16 17 18 – DCI – 09 08 07 06 05

*C*ontents

Continued

Pygmalion

Bernard Shaw

Preface

A Professor of Phonetics

As will be seen later on, Pygmalion needs, not a preface, but a sequel, which I have supplied in its due place.

The English have no respect for their language, and will not teach their children to speak it. They cannot spell it because they have nothing to spell it with but an old foreign alphabet of which only the consonants—and not all of them—have any agreed speech value. Consequently no man can teach himself what it should sound like from reading it; and it is impossible for an Englishman to open his mouth without making some other Englishman despise him. Most European languages are now accessible in black and white to foreigners: English and French are not thus accessible even to Englishmen and Frenchmen. The reformer we need most today is an energetic phonetic enthusiast: that is why I have made such a one the hero of a popular play.

There have been heroes of that kind crying in the wilderness for many years past. When I became interested in the subject towards the end of the eighteen-seventies, the illustrious Alexander Melville Bell, the inventor of Visible Speech, had emigrated to Canada, where his son invented the telephone; but Alexander J. Ellis was still a London patriarch, with an impressive head always covered by a velvet skull cap, for which he would apologize to public meetings in a very courtly manner. He and Tito Pagliardini, another phonetic veteran, were men whom it was impossible to dislike. Henry Sweet, then a young man, lacked their sweetness of character: he was about as conciliatory to conventional mortals as Ibsen or Samuel Butler. His great ability as a phonetician (he was, I think, the best of them all at his job) would have entitled him to high official recognition, and perhaps enabled him to popularize his subject, but for his Satanic contempt for all academic dignitaries and persons in general who thought more of Greek than of phonetics. Once, in the days when the Imperial Institute rose in South Kensington, and Joseph Chamberlain was booming the Empire, I induced the editor of a leading monthly review to commission an article from Sweet on the imperial importance of his subject. When it arrived, it contained nothing but a savagely derisive attack on a professor of language and literature whose chair Sweet regarded as proper to a phonetic expert only. The article, being libellous, had to be returned as impossible; and I had to renounce my dream of dragging its author into the limelight. When I met him afterwards, for the first time for many years, I found to my astonishment that he, who had been a quite tolerably presentable young man, had actually managed by sheer scorn to alter his personal appearance until he had become a sort of walking repudiation of Oxford and all its traditions. It must have been largely in his own despite that he was squeezed into something called a Readership of phonetics there. The future of phonetics rests probably with his pupils, who all swore by him; but nothing could bring the man himself into any sort of compliance with the university to which he nevertheless clung by divine right in an intensely Oxonian way. I daresay his papers, if he has left any, include some satires that may be published without too destructive results fifty years hence. He was, I believe, not in the least an ill-natured man: very much the opposite, I should say; but he would not suffer fools gladly; and to him all scholars who were not rabid phoneticians were fools.

Those who knew him will recognize in my third act the allusion to the Current Shorthand in which he used to write postcards. It may be acquired from a four and sixpenny manual published by the Clarendon Press. The postcards which Mrs. Higgins describes are such as I have received from Sweet. I would decipher a sound which a cockney would represent by *zerr,* and a Frenchman by *seu,* and then write demanding with some heat what on earth it meant. Sweet, with boundless contempt for my stupidity, would reply that it not only meant but obviously was the word Result, as no other word containing that sound, and capable of making sense with the context, existed in any language spoken on earth. That less expert mortals should require fuller indications was beyond Sweet's patience. Therefore, though the whole point of his Current Shorthand is that it can express every sound in the language perfectly, vowels as well as consonants, and that your hand has to make no stroke except the easy and current one with which you write m, n, and u, l, p, and q, scribbling them at whatever angle comes easiest to you, his unfortunate determination to make this remarkable and quite legible script serve also as a shorthand reduced it in his own practice to the most inscrutable of cryptograms. His true objective was the provision of a full, accurate, legible script for our language; but he was led past that by his contempt for the popular Pitman system of shorthand, which he called the Pitfall system. The triumph of Pitman was a triumph of business organization: there was a weekly paper to persuade you to learn Pitman: there were cheap textbooks and exercise books and transcripts of speeches for you to copy, and schools where experienced teachers coached you up to the necessary proficiency. Sweet could not organize his market in that fashion. He might as well have been the Sybil who tore up the leaves of prophecy that nobody would attend to. The four and sixpenny manual, mostly in his lithographed handwriting, that was never vulgarly advertized, may perhaps some day be taken up by a syndicate and pushed upon the public as The Times pushed the Encyclopædia Britannica; but until then it will certainly not prevail against Pitman. I have bought three copies of it during my lifetime; and I am informed by the publishers that its cloistered existence is still a steady and healthy one. I actually learned the system two several times; and yet the shorthand in which I am writing these lines is Pitman's. And the reason is, that my secretary cannot transcribe Sweet, having been perforce taught in the schools of Pitman. In America I could use the commercially organized Gregg shorthand, which has taken a hint from Sweet by making its letters writable (current, Sweet would have called them) instead of having to be geometrically drawn like Pitman's; but all these systems, including Sweet's, are spoilt by making them available for verbatim reporting, in which complete and exact spelling and word division are impossible. A complete and exact phonetic script is neither practicable nor necessary for ordinary use; but if we enlarge our alphabet to the Russian size, and make our spelling as phonetic as Spanish, the advance will be prodigious.

Pygmalion Higgins is not a portrait of Sweet, to whom the adventure of Eliza Doolittle would have been impossible; still, as will be seen, there are touches of Sweet in the play. With Higgins's physique and temperament Sweet might have set the Thames on fire. As it was, he impressed himself professionally on Europe to an extent that made his comparative personal obscurity, and the failure of Oxford to do justice to his eminence, a puzzle to foreign specialists in his subject. I do not blame Oxford, because I think Oxford is quite right in demanding a certain social amenity from its nurslings (heaven knows it is not exorbitant in its requirements!); for although I well know how hard it is for a man of genius with a seriously underrated subject to maintain serene and kindly relations with the men who underrate it, and who keep all the best places for less important subjects which they profess without originality and sometimes without much capacity for them, still, if he overwhelms them with wrath and disdain, he cannot expect them to heap honors on him.

Of the later generations of phoneticians I know little. Among them towered Robert Bridges, to whom perhaps Higgins may owe his Miltonic sympathies, though here again I must disclaim all portraiture. But if the play makes the public aware that there are such people as phoneticians, and that they are among the most important people in England at present, it will serve its turn.

I wish to boast that Pygmalion has been an extremely successful play, both on stage and screen, all over Europe and North America as well as at home. It is so intensely and deliberately didactic, and its subject is esteemed so dry, that I delight in throwing it at the heads of the wiseacres who repeat the parrot cry that art should never be didactic. It goes to prove my contention that great art can never be anything else.

Finally, and for the encouragement of people troubled with accents that cut them off from all high employment, I may add that the change wrought by Professor Higgins in the flower-girl is neither impossible nor uncommon. The modern concierge's daughter who fulfils her ambition by playing the Queen of Spain in Ruy Blas at the Théâtre Français is only one of many thousands of men and women who have sloughed off their native dialects and acquired a new tongue. Our West End shop assistants and domestic servants are bilingual. But the thing has to be done scientifically, or the last state of the aspirant may be worse than the first. An honest slum dialect is more tolerable than the attempts of phonetically untaught persons to imitate the plutocracy. Ambitions flower-girls who read this play must not imagine that they can pass themselves off as fine ladies by untutored imitation. They must learn their alphabet over again, and different, from a phonetic expert. Imitation will only make them ridiculous.

Act ONE

London at 11.15 P.M. Torrents of heavy summer rain. Cab whistles blowing frantically in all directions. Pedestrians running for shelter into the portico of St Paul's church (not Wren's cathedral but Inigo Jones's church in Covent Garden vegetable market), among them a lady and her daughter in evening dress. All are peering out gloomily at the rain, except one man with his back turned to the rest, wholly preoccupied with a notebook in which he is writing.

The church clock strikes the first quarter.

The Daughter (*in the space between the central pillars, close to the one on her left*). I'm getting chilled to the bone. What can Freddy be doing all this time? He's been gone twenty minutes.

The Mother (*on her daughter's right*). Not so long. But he ought to have got us a cab by this.

A Bystander (*on the lady's right*). He won't get no cab not until half-past eleven, missus, when they come back after dropping their theatre fares.

The Mother. But we must have a cab. We can't stand here until half-past eleven. It's too bad.

The Bystander. Well it ain't my fault, missus.

The Daughter. If Freddy had a bit of gumption, he would have got one at the theatre door.

The Mother. What could he have done, poor boy?

The Daughter. Other people get cabs. Why couldn't he?

Freddy rushes in out of the rain from the Southampton Street side, and comes between them closing a dripping umbrella. He is a young man of twenty, in evening dress, very wet round the ankles.

The Daughter. Well, havn't you got a cab?

Freddy. Theres not one to be had for love or money.

The Mother. Oh, Freddy, there must be one. You can't have tried.

The Daughter. It's too tiresome. Do you expect us to go and get one ourselves?

Freddy. I tell you theyre all engaged. The rain was so sudden: nobody was prepared; and everybody had to take a cab. I've been to Charing Cross one way and nearly to Ludgate Circus the other; and they were all engaged.

The Mother. Did you try Trafalgar Square?

Freddy. There wasn't one at Trafalgar Square.

The Daughter. Did you try?

Freddy. I tried as far as Charing Cross Station. Did you expect me to walk to Hammersmith?

The Daughter. You havn't tried at all.

The Mother. You really are very helpless, Freddy. Go again; and don't come back until you have found a cab.

Freddy. I shall simply get soaked for nothing.

The Daughter. And what about us? Are we to stay here all night in this draught, with next to nothing on? You selfish pig—

Freddy. Oh, very well: I'll go, I'll go. (*He opens his umbrella and dashes off Strandwards, but comes into collision with a flower girl who is hurrying in for shelter, knocking her basket out of her hands. A blinding flash of lightning, followed instantly by a rattling peal of thunder, orchestrates the incident*).

The Flower Girl. Nah then, Freddy: look wh' y' gowin, deah.

Freddy. Sorry (*he rushes off*).

The Flower Girl (*picking up her scattered flowers and replacing them in the basket*). Theres menners f' yer! Tə-oo banches o voylets trod into the mad. (*She sits down on the plinth of the column, sorting her flowers, on the lady's right. She is not at all a romantic figure. She is perhaps eighteen, perhaps twenty, hardly older. She wears a little sailor hat of black straw that has long been exposed to the dust and soot of London and has seldom if ever been brushed. Her hair needs washing rather badly: its mousy color can hardly be natural. She wears a shoddy black coat that reaches nearly to her knees and is shaped to her waist. She has a brown skirt with a coarse apron. Her boots are much the worse for wear. She is no doubt as clean as she can afford to be; but compared to the ladies she is very dirty. Her features are no worse than theirs; but their condition leaves something to be desired; and she needs the services of a dentist.*)

The Mother. How do you know that my son's name is Freddy, pray?

The Flower Girl. Ow, eez, yə-ooa san, is e? Wal, fewd dan y' d-ooty bawmz a mather should, eed now bettern to spawl a pore gel's flahzrn than ran awy athaht pyin. Will ye-oo py me f'them? (*Here, with apologies, this desperate attempt to represent her dialect without a phonetic alphabet must be abandoned as unintelligible outside London.*)

The Daughter. Do nothing of the sort, mother. The idea!

The Mother. Please allow me, Clara. Have you any pennies?

The Daughter. No. I've nothing smaller than sixpence.

The Flower Girl (*hopefully*). I can give you change for a tanner, kind lady.

The Mother (*to* Clara). Give it to me. (*Clara parts reluctantly.*) Now (*to the girl*) This is for your flowers.

The Flower Girl. Thank you kindly, lady.

The Daughter. Make her give you the change. These things are only a penny a bunch.

The Mother. Do hold your tongue, Clara. (*To the girl*) You can keep the change.

The Flower Girl. Oh, thank you, lady.

The Mother. Now tell me how you know that young gentleman's name.

The Flower Girl. I didn't.

The Mother. I heard you call him by it. Don't try to deceive me.

The Flower Girl (*protesting*). Who's trying to deceive you? I called him Freddy or Charlie same as you might yourself if you was talking to a stranger and wished to be pleasant.

The Daughter. Sixpence thrown away! Really, mamma, you might have spared Freddy that. (*She retreats in disgust behind the pillar.*)

An elderly gentleman of the amiable military type rushes into the shelter, and closes a dripping umbrella. He is in the same plight as Freddy, very wet about the ankles. He is in evening dress, with a light overcoat. He takes the place left vacant by the daughter.

The Gentleman. Phew!

The Mother (*to the gentleman*). Oh, sir, is there any sign of its stopping?

The Gentleman. I'm afraid not. It started worse than ever about two minutes ago (*he goes to the plinth beside the flower girl; puts up his foot on it; and stoops to turn down his trouser ends.*)

The Mother. Oh dear! (*She retires sadly and joins her daughter.*)

The Flower Girl (*taking advantage of the military gentleman's proximity to establish friendly relations with him*). If it's worse, it's a sign it's nearly over. So cheer up, Captain; and buy a flower off a poor girl.

The Gentleman. I'm sorry. I havn't any change.

The Flower Girl. I can give you change, Captain.

The Gentleman. For a sovereign? I've nothing less.

The Flower Girl. Garn! Oh do buy a flower off me, Captain. I can change half-a-crown. Take this for tuppence.

The Gentleman. Now don't be troublesome: theres a good girl. (*Trying his pockets*) I really havn't any change—Stop: heres three hapence, if thats any use to you (*he retreats to the other pillar.*)

The Flower Girl (*disappointed, but thinking three halfpence better than nothing*). Thank you, sir.

The Bystander (*to the girl*). You be careful: give him a flower for it. Theres a bloke here behind taking down every blessed word youre saying. (*All turn to the man who is taking notes.*)

The Flower Girl (*springing up terrified*). I ain't done nothing wrong by speaking to the gentleman. I've a right to sell flowers if I keep off the kerb. (*Hysterically*) I'm a respectable girl: so help me, I never spoke to him except to ask him to buy a flower off me.

General hubbub, mostly sympathetic to the flower girl, but deprecating her excessive sensibility. Cries of Don't start hollerin. Who's hurting you? Nobody's going to touch you. Whats the good of fussing? Steady on. Easy easy, etc., *come from the elderly staid spectators, who pat her comfortingly. Less patient ones bid her shut her head, or ask her roughly what is wrong with her. A remoter group, not knowing what the matter is, crowd in and increase the noise with question and answer:* Whats the row? What-she-do? Where is he? A tec taking her down. What! him? Yes: him over there: Took money off the gentleman, etc.

The Flower Girl (*breaking through them to the gentleman, crying wildly*). Oh, sir, don't let him charge me. You dunno what it means to me. Theyll take away my character and drive me on the streets for speaking to gentlemen. They—

The Note Taker (*coming forward on her right, the rest crowding after him*). There! there! there! there! who's hurting you, you silly girl? What do you take me for?

The Bystander. It's aw rawt: e's a gentleman: look at his bə-oots. (*Explaining to the note taker*) She thought you was a copper's nark, sir.

The Note Taker (*with quick interest*). Whats a copper's nark?

The Bystander (*inapt at definition*). It's a—well, it's a copper's nark, as you might say. What else would you call it? A sort of informer.

The Flower Girl (*still hysterical*). I take my Bible oath I never said a word—

The Note Taker (*overbearing but good-humored*). Oh, shut up, shut up. Do I look like a policeman?

The Flower Girl (*far from reassured*). Then what did you take down my words for? How do I know whether you took me down right? You just shew me what youve wrote about me. (*The note taker opens his book and holds it steadily under her nose, though the pressure of the mob trying to read it over his shoulders would upset a weaker man.*) What's that? That ain't proper writing. I can't read that.

The Note Taker. I can. (*Reads, reproducing her pronunciation exactly*) "Cheer ap, Keptin; n' baw ya flahr orf a pore gel."

The Flower Girl (*much distressed*). It's because I called him Captain. I meant no harm. (*To the gentleman*) Oh, sir, don't let him lay a charge agen me for a word like that. You—

The Gentleman. Charge! I make no charge. (*To the note taker*) Really, sir, if you are a detective, you need not begin protecting me against molestation by young women until I ask you. Anybody could see that the girl meant no harm.

The Bystanders Generally (*demonstrating against police espionage*). Course they could. What business is it of yours? You mind your own affairs. He wants promotion, he does. Taking down people's words! Girl never said a word to him. What harm if she did? Nice thing a girl can't shelter from the rain without being insulted, etc., etc., etc. (*She is conducted by the more sympathetic demonstrators back to her plinth, where she resumes her seat and struggles with her emotion.*)

The Bystander. He ain't a tec. He's a blooming busy-body: thats what he is. I tell you, look at his bə-oots.

The Note Taker (*turning on him genially*). And how are all your people down at Selsey?

The Bystander (*suspiciously*). Who told you my people come from Selsey?

The Note Taker. Never you mind. They did. (*To the girl*) How do you come to be up so far east? You were born in Lisson Grove.

The Flower Girl (*appalled*). Oh, what harm is there in my leaving Lisson Grove? It wasn't fit for a pig to live in; and I had to pay four-and-six a week. (*In tears*) Oh, boo—hoo—oo—

The Note Taker. Live where you like; but stop that noise.

The Gentleman (*to the girl*). Come, come! he can't touch you: you have a right to live where you please.

A Sarcastic Bystander (*thrusting himself between the note taker and the gentleman*). Park Lane, for instance. I'd like to go into the Housing Question with you, I would.

The Flower Girl (*subsiding into a brooding melancholy over her basket, and talking very low-spiritedly to herself*). I'm a good girl, I am.

The Sarcastic Bystander (*not attending to her*). Do you know where I come from?

The Note Taker (*promptly*). Hoxton.

Titterings. Popular interest in the note taker's performance increases.

The Sarcastic One (*amazed*). Well, who said I didnt? Bly me! you know everything, you do.

The Flower Girl (*still nursing her sense of injury*). Ain't no call to meddle with me, he aint.

The Bystander (*to her*). Of course he aint. Don't you stand it from him. (*To the note taker*) See here: what call have you to know about people what never offered to meddle with you?

The Flower Girl. Let him say what he likes. I don't want to have no truck with him.

The Bystander. You take us for dirt under your feet, don't you? Catch you taking liberties with a gentleman!

The Sarcastic Bystander. Yes: tell him where he come from if you want to go fortune-telling.

The Note Taker. Cheltenham. Harrow, Cambridge, and India.

The Gentleman. Quite right.

Great laughter. Reaction in the note taker's favor. Exclamations of He knows all about it. Told him proper. Hear him tell the toff where he come from? *etc.*

The Gentleman. May I ask, sir, do you do this for your living at a music hall?

The Note Taker. I've thought of that. Perhaps I shall some day.

The rain has stopped; and the persons on the outside of the crowd begin to drop off.

The Flower Girl (*resenting the reaction*). He's no gentleman, he ain't, to interfere with a poor girl.

The Daughter (*out of patience, pushing her way rudely to* the front and displacing the gentleman, who politely retires to the other side of the pillar). What on earth is Freddy doing? I shall get pneumownia if I stay in this draught any longer.

The Note Taker (to himself, hastily making a note of her pronunciation of 'monia'). Earlscourt.

The Daughter (violently). Will you please keep your impertinent remarks to yourself.

The Note Taker. Did I say that out loud? I didn't mean to. I beg your pardon. Your mother's Epsom, unmistakeably.

The Mother (advancing between the daughter and the note taker). How very curious! I was brought up in Largelady Park, near Epsom.

The Note Taker (uproariously amused). Ha! ha! what a devil of a name! Excuse me. (To the daughter) You want a cab, do you?

The Daughter. Don't dare speak to me.

The Mother. Oh, please, please, Clara. (Her daughter repudiates her with an angry shrug and retires haughtily.) We should be so grateful to you, sir, if you found us a cab. (The note taker produces a whistle). Oh, thank you. (She joins her daughter.)

The note taker blows a piercing blast.

The Sarcastic Bystander. There! I knowed he was a plainclothes copper.

The Bystander. That ain't a police whistle: thats a sporting whistle.

The Flower Girl (still preoccupied with her wounded feelings). He's no right to take away my character. My character is the same to me as any lady's.

The Note Taker. I don't know whether youve noticed it; but the rain stopped about two minutes ago.

The Bystander. So it has. Why didn't you say so before? and us losing our time listening to your silliness! (*He walks off towards the Strand.*)

The Sarcastic Bystander. I can tell where you come from. You come from Anwell. Go back there.

The Note Taker (*helpfully*). *H*anwell.

The Sarcastic Bystander (*affecting great distinction of speech*). Thenk you, teacher. Haw haw! So long (*he touches his hat with mock respect and strolls off*).

The Flower Girl. Frightening people like that! How would he like it himself?

The Mother. It's quite fine now, Clara. We can walk to a motor bus. Come. (*She gathers her skirts above her ankles and hurries off towards the Strand.*)

The Daughter. But the cab—(*her mother is out of hearing*). Oh, how tiresome! (*She follows angrily.*)

All the rest have gone except the note taker, the gentleman, and the flower girl, who sits arranging her basket, and still pitying herself in murmurs.

The Flower Girl. Poor girl! Hard enough for her to live without being worrited and chivied.

The Gentleman (*returning to his former place on the note taker's left*). How do you do it, if I may ask?

The Note Taker. Simply phonetics. The science of speech. Thats my profession: also my hobby. Happy is the man who can make a living by his hobby! You can spot an Irishman or a Yorkshireman by his brogue. *I* can place any man within six miles. I can place him within two miles in London. Sometimes within two streets.

The Flower Girl. Ought to be ashamed of himself, unmanly coward!

The Gentleman. But is there a living in that?

The Note Taker. Oh, yes. Quite a fat one. This is an age of upstarts. Men begin in Kentish Town with £80 a year, and end in Park Lane with a hundred thousand. They want to drop Kentish Town; but they give themselves away every time they open their mouths. Now I can teach them—

The Flower Girl. Let him mind his own business and leave a poor girl—

The Note Taker (*explosively*). Woman: cease this detestable boohooing instantly; or else seek the shelter of some other place of worship.

The Flower Girl (*with feeble defiance*). I've a right to be here if I like, same as you.

The Note Taker. A woman who utters such depressing and disgusting sounds has no right to be anywhere— no right to live. Remember that you are a human being with a soul and the divine gift of articulate speech: that your native language is the language of Shakespear and Milton and The Bible; and don't sit there crooning like a bilious pigeon.

The Flower Girl (*quite overwhelmed, looking up at him in mingled wonder and deprecation without daring to raise her head*). Ah-ah-ah-ow-ow-ow-oo!

The Note Taker (*whipping out his book*). Heavens! what a sound! (*He writes; then holds out the book and reads, reproducing her vowels exactly*) Ah-ah-ah-ow-ow-ow-oo!

The Flower Girl (*tickled by the performance, and laughing in spite of herself*). Garn!

The Note Taker. You see this creature with her kerb-stone English: the English that will keep her in the gutter to the end of her days. Well, sir, in three months I could pass that girl off as a duchess at an ambassador's garden party. I could even get her a place as lady's maid or shop assistant, which requires better English.

The Flower Girl. What's that you say?

The Note Taker. Yes, you squashed cabbage leaf, you disgrace to the noble architecture of these columns, you incarnate insult to the English language. I could pass you off as the Queen of Sheba. (*To the Gentleman*) Can you believe that?

The Gentleman. Of course I can. I am myself a student of Indian dialects; and—

The Note Taker (*eagerly*). Are you? Do you know Colonel Pickering, the author of Spoken Sanscrit?

The Gentleman. I am Colonel Pickering. Who are you?

The Note Taker. Henry Higgins, author of Higgins's Universal Alphabet.

Pickering (*with enthusiasm*). I came from India to meet you.

Higgins. I was going to India to meet you.

Pickering. Where do you live?

Higgins. 27A Wimpole Street. Come and see me tomorrow.

Pickering. I'm at the Carlton. Come with me now and lets have a jaw over some supper.

Higgins. Right you are.

The Flower Girl (*to Pickering, as he passes her*). Buy a flower, kind gentleman. I'm short for my lodging.

Pickering. I really havn't any change. I'm sorry (*he goes away*).

Higgins (*shocked at the girl's mendacity*). Liar. You said you could change half-a-crown.

The Flower Girl (*rising in desperation*). You ought to be stuffed with nails, you ought. (*Flinging the basket at his feet*) Take the whole blooming basket for sixpence.

The church clock strikes the second quarter.

Higgins (*hearing in it the voice of God, rebuking him for his Pharisaic want of charity to the poor girl*). A reminder. (*He raises his hat solemnly; then throws a handful of money into the basket and follows* Pickering.)

The Flower Girl (*picking up a half-crown*). Ah-ow-ooh! (*Picking up a couple of florins*) Aaah-ow-ooh! (*Picking up several coins*) Aaaaaah-ow-ooh! (*Picking up a half-sovereign*) Aaaaaaaaaaaah-ow-ooh!!!

Freddy (*springing out of a taxicab*). Got one at last. Hallo! (*To the girl*) Where are the two ladies that were here?

The Flower Girl. They walked to the bus when the rain stopped.

Freddy. And left me with a cab on my hands! Damnation!

The Flower Girl (*with grandeur*). Never mind, young man. *I*'m going home in a taxi. (*She sails off to the cab. The driver puts his hand behind him and holds the door firmly shut against her. Quite understanding his mistrust, she shews him her handful of money.*) A taxi fare ain't no object to me, Charlie. (*He grins and opens the door.*) Here. What about the basket?

The Taximan. Give it here. Tuppence extra.

Liza. No: I don't want nobody to see it. (*She crushes it into the cab and gets in, continuing the conversation through the window.*) Goodbye, Freddy.

Freddy (*dazedly raising his hat*). Goodbye.

Taximan. Where to?

Liza. Bucknam Pellis (*Buckingham Palace*).

Taximan. What d'ye mean—Bucknam Pellis?

Liza. Don't you know where it is? In the Green Park, where the King lives. Goodbye, Freddy. Dont let me keep you standing there. Goodbye.

Freddy. Goodbye. (*He goes*).

Taximan. Here? Whats this about Bucknam Pellis? What business have you at Bucknam Pellis?

Liza. Of course I havn't none. But I wasn't going to let him know that. You drive me home.

Taximan. And wheres home?

Liza. Angel Court, Drury Lane, next Meiklejohn's oil shop.

Taximan. That sounds more like it, Judy. (*He drives off.*)

Let us follow the taxi to the entrance to Angel Court, a narrow little archway between two shops, one of them Meiklejohn's oil shop. When it stops there, Eliza *gets out, dragging her basket with her.*

Liza. How much?

Taximan (*indicating the taximeter*). Can't you read? A shilling.

Liza. A shilling for two minutes!!

Taximan. Two minutes or ten: it's all the same.

Liza. Well, I don't call it right.

Taximan. Ever been in a taxi before?

Liza (*with dignity*). Hundreds and thousands of times, young man.

Taximan (*laughing at her*). Good for you, Judy. Keep the shilling, darling, with best love from all at home. Good luck! (*He drives off.*)

Liza (*humiliated*). Impidence!

She picks up the basket and trudges up the alley with it to her lodging: a small room with very old wall paper hanging loose in the damp places. A broken pane in the window is mended with paper. A portrait of a popular actor and a fashion plate of ladies' dresses, all wildly beyond poor Eliza's means, both torn from newspapers, are pinned up on the wall. A birdcage hangs in the window; but its tenant died long ago: it remains as a memorial only.

These are the only visible luxuries: the rest is the irreducible minimum of poverty's needs: a wretched bed heaped with all sorts of coverings that have any warmth in them, a draped packing case with a basin and jug on it and a little looking glass over it, a chair and table, the refuse of some suburban kitchen, and an American alarum clock on the shelf above the unused fireplace: the whole lighted with a gas lamp with a penny in the slot meter. Rent: four shillings a week.

Here Eliza, *chronically weary, but too excited to go to bed, sits, counting her new riches and dreaming and planning what to do with them, until the gas goes out, when she enjoys for the first time the sensation of being able to put in another penny without grudging it. This prodigal mood does not extinguish her gnawing sense of the need for economy sufficiently to prevent her from calculating that she can dream and plan in bed more cheaply and warmly than sitting up without a fire. So she takes off her shawl and skirt and adds them to the miscellaneous bedclothes. Then she kicks off her shoes and gets into bed without any further change.*

Act TWO

Next day at 11 A.M. Higgins's laboratory in Wimpole Street. It is a room on the first floor, looking on the street, and was meant for the drawing room. The double doors are in the middle of the back wall; and persons entering find in the corner to their right two tall file cabinets at right angles to one another against the wall. In this corner stands a flat writing-table, on which are a phonograph, a laryngoscope, a row of tiny organ pipes with a bellows, a set of lamp chimneys for singing flames with burners attached to a gas plug in the wall by an indiarubber tube, several tuning-forks of different sizes, a life-size image of half a human head, shewing in section the vocal organs, and a box containing a supply of wax cylinders for the phonograph.

Further down the room, on the same side, is a fireplace, with a comfortable leather-covered easy-chair at the side of the hearth nearest the door, and a coal-scuttle. There is a clock on the mantelpiece. Between the fireplace and the phonograph table is a stand for newspapers.

On the other side of the central door, to the left of the visitor, is a cabinet of shallow drawers. On it is a telephone and the telephone directory. The corner beyond, and most of the side wall, is occupied by a grand piano, with the keyboard at the end furthest from the door, and a bench for the player extending the full length of the keyboard. On the piano is a dessert dish heaped with fruit and sweets, mostly chocolates.

*The middle of the room is clear. Besides
the easy-chair, the piano bench, and two
chairs at the phonograph table, there is
one stray chair. It stands near the fireplace.
On the walls, engravings: mostly Piranesis
and mezzotint portraits. No paintings.*

Pickering *is seated at the table, putting
down some cards and a tuning-fork which
he has been using. Higgins is standing up
near him, closing two or three file drawers
which are hanging out. He appears in the
morning light as a robust, vital, appetizing
sort of man of forty or thereabouts,
dressed in a professional-looking black
frock-coat with a white linen collar and
black silk tie. He is of the energetic
scientific type, heartily, even violently
interested in everything that can be
studied as a scientific subject, and careless
about himself and other people, including
their feelings. He is, in fact, but for his
years and size, rather like a very
impetuous baby 'taking notice' eagerly
and loudly, and requiring almost as much
watching to keep him out of unintended
mischief. His manner varies from genial
bullying when he is in a good humor to
stormy petulance when anything goes
wrong; but he is so entirely frank and void
of malice that he remains likeable even in
his least reasonable moments.*

Higgins (*as he shuts the last drawer*). Well, I think thats
the whole show.

Pickering. It's really amazing. I havn't taken half of it
in, you know.

Higgins. Would you like to go over any of it again?

Pickering (*rising and coming to the fireplace, where he
plants himself with his back to the fire*). No, thank you:

not now. I'm quite done up for this morning.

Higgins (*following him, and standing beside him on his left*). Tired of listening to sounds?

Pickering. Yes. It's a fearful strain. I rather fancied myself because I can pronounce twenty-four distinct vowel sounds; but your hundred and thirty beat me. I can't hear a bit of difference between most of them.

Higgins (*chuckling, and going over to the piano to eat sweets*). Oh, that comes with practice. You hear no difference at first; but you keep on listening, and presently you find theyre all as different as A from B. (Mrs. Pearce *looks in: she is* Higgins's *housekeeper*.) Whats the matter?

Mrs. Pearce (*hesitating, evidently perplexed*). A young woman asks to see you, sir.

Higgins. A young woman! What does she want?

Mrs. Pearce. Well, sir, she says youll be glad to see her when you know what she's come about. She's quite a common girl, sir. Very common indeed. I should have sent her away, only I thought perhaps you wanted her to talk into your machines. I hope I've not done wrong; but really you see such queer people sometimes—youll excuse me, I'm sure, sir—

Higgins. Oh, thats all right, Mrs. Pearce. Has she an interesting accent?

Mrs. Pearce. Oh, something dreadful, sir, really. I don't know how you can take an interest in it.

Higgins (*to* Pickering). Lets have her up. Shew her up, Mrs. Pearce (*he rushes across to his working table and picks out a cylinder to use on the phonograph*).

Mrs. Pearce (*only half resigned to it*). Very well, sir. It's for you to say. (*She goes downstairs.*)

Higgins. This is rather a bit of luck. I'll shew you how I make records. We'll set her talking; and I'll take it down first in Bell's Visible Speech; then in broad Romic; and then we'll get her on the phonograph so that you can turn her on as often as you like with the written transcript before you.

Mrs. Pearce (*returning*). This is the young woman, sir.

The flower girl enters in state. She has a hat with three ostrich feathers, orange, sky-blue, and red. She has a nearly clean apron and the shoddy coat has been tidied a little. The pathos of this deplorable figure, with its innocent vanity and consequential air, touches Pickering, *who has already straightened himself in the presence of* Mrs. Pearce. *But as to* Higgins, *the only distinction he makes between men and women is that when he is neither bullying nor exclaiming to the heavens against some featherweight cross, he coaxes women as a child coaxes its nurse when it wants to get anything out of her.*

Higgins (*brusquely, recognizing her with unconcealed disappointment, and at once, babylike, making an intolerable grievance of it*). Why, this is the girl I jotted down last night. She's no use: I've got all the records I want of the Lisson Grove lingo; and I'm not going to waste another cylinder on it. (*To the girl*) Be off with you: I don't want you.

The Flower Girl. Don't you be so saucy. You ain't heard what I come for yet. (*To* Mrs. Pearce, *who is waiting at the door for further instructions*) Did you tell him I come in a taxi?

Mrs. Pearce. Nonsense, girl! what do you think a gentleman like Mr. Higgins cares what you came in?

The Flower Girl. Oh, we are proud! He ain't above giving lessons, not him: I heard him say so. Well, I ain't come here to ask for any compliment; and if my money's not good enough I can go elsewhere.

Higgins. Good enough for what?

The Flower Girl. Good enough for yə-oo. Now you know, don't you? I'm coming to have lessons, I am. And to pay for em tə-oo: make no mistake.

Higgins (*stupent*). Well!!! (*Recovering his breath with a gasp*) What do you expect me to say to you?

The Flower Girl. Well, if you was a gentleman, you might ask me to sit down, I think. Don't I tell you I'm bringing you business?

Higgins. Pickering: shall we ask this baggage to sit down, or shall we throw her out of the window?

The Flower Girl (*running away in terror to the piano, where she turns at bay*). Ah-ah-oh-ow-ow-ow-oo! (*Wounded and whimpering*) I won't be called a baggage when I've offered to pay like any lady.

Motionless, the two men stare at her from the other side of the room, amazed.

Pickering (*gently*). But what is it you want?

The Flower Girl. I want to be a lady in a flower shop stead of sellin at the corner of Tottenham Court Road. But they won't take me unless I can talk more genteel. He said he could teach me. Well, here I am ready to pay him—not asking any favor—and he treats me zif I was dirt.

Mrs. Pearce. How can you be such a foolish ignorant girl as to think you could afford to pay Mr. Higgins?

The Flower Girl. Why shouldn't I? I know what lessons cost as well as you do; and I'm ready to pay.

Higgins. How much?

The Flower Girl (*coming back to him, triumphant*). Now youre talking! I thought youd come off it when you saw a chance of getting back a bit of what you chucked at me last night. (*Confidentially*) Youd had a drop in, hadn't you?

Higgins (*peremptorily*). Sit down.

The Flower Girl. Oh, if youre going to make a compliment of it—

Higgins (*thundering at her*). Sit down.

Mrs. Pearce (*severely*). Sit down, girl. Do as youre told.

The Flower Girl. Ah-ah-ah-ow-ow-oo! (*She stands, half rebellious, half-bewildered.*)

Pickering (*very courteous*). Won't you sit down? (*He places the stray chair near the hearthrug between himself and* Higgins.)

Liza (*coyly*). Don't mind if I do. (*She sits down.* Pickering *returns to the hearthrug.*)

Higgins. Whats your name?

The Flower Girl. Liza Doolittle.

Higgins (*declaiming gravely*).

Eliza, Elizabeth, Betsy and Bess,
They went to the woods to get a bird's nes':

Pickering. They found a nest with four eggs in it:

Higgins. They took one apiece, and left three in it.

They laugh heartily at their own fun.

Liza. Oh, don't be silly.

Mrs. Pearce (*placing herself behind* Eliza's *chair*). You mustn't speak to the gentleman like that.

Liza. Well, why won't he speak sensible to me?

Higgins. Come back to business. How much do you propose to pay me for the lessons?

Liza. Oh, I know whats right. A lady friend of mine gets French lessons for eighteenpence an hour from a real French gentleman. Well, you wouldn't have the face to ask me the same for teaching me my own language as you would for French; so I won't give more than a shilling. Take it or leave it.

Higgins (*walking up and down the room, rattling his keys and his cash in his pockets*). You know, Pickering, if you consider a shilling, not as a simple shilling, but as a percentage of this girl's income, it works out as fully equivalent to sixty or seventy guineas from a millionaire.

Pickering. How so?

Higgins. Figure it out. A millionaire has about £150 a day. She earns about half-a-crown.

Liza (*haughtily*). Who told you I only—

Higgins (*continuing*). She offers me two-fifths of her day's income for a lesson. Two-fifths of a millionaire's income for a day would be somewhere about £60. It's handsome. By George, it's enormous! it's the biggest offer I ever had.

Liza (*rising, terrified*). Sixty pounds! What are you talking about? I never offered you sixty pounds. Where would I get—

Higgins. Hold your tongue.

Liza (*weeping*). But I ain't got sixty pounds. Oh—

Mrs. Pearce. Don't cry, you silly girl. Sit down. Nobody is going to touch your money.

Higgins. Somebody is going to touch you, with a broomstick, if you don't stop snivelling. Sit down.

Liza (*obeying slowly*). Ah-ah-ah-ow-oo-o! One would think you was my father.

Higgins. If I decide to teach you, I'll be worse than two fathers to you. Here (*he offers her his silk handkerchief*)!

Liza. Whats this for?

Higgins. To wipe your eyes. To wipe any part of your face that feels moist. Remember: thats your handkerchief; and thats your sleeve. Don't mistake the one for the other if you wish to become a lady in a shop.

Liza, *utterly bewildered, stares helplessly at him.*

Mrs. Pearce. It's no use talking to her like that, Mr. Higgins: she doesn't understand you. Besides, youre quite wrong: she doesn't do it that way at all (*she takes the handkerchief*).

Liza (*snatching it*). Here! You give me that handkerchief. He gev it to me, not to you.

Pickering (*laughing*). He did. I think it must be regarded as her property, Mrs. Pearce.

Mrs. Pearce (*resigning herself*). Serve you right, Mr. Higgins.

Pickering. Higgins: I'm interested. What about the ambassador's garden party? I'll say youre the greatest teacher alive if you make that good. I'll bet you all the expenses of the experiment you can't do it. And I'll pay for the lessons.

Liza. Oh, you are real good. Thank you, Captain.

Higgins (*tempted, looking at her*). It's almost irresistible.

She's so deliciously low—so horribly dirty—

Liza (*protesting extremely*). Ah-ah-ah-ah-ow-ow-oo-oo!!! I ain't dirty: I washed my face and hands afore I come, I did.

Pickering. Youre certainly not going to turn her head with flattery, Higgins.

Mrs. Pearce (*uneasy*). Oh, don't say that, sir: theres more ways than one of turning a girl's head; and nobody can do it better than Mr. Higgins, though he may not always mean it. I do hope, sir, you wont encourage him to do anything foolish.

Higgins (*becoming excited as the idea grows on him*). What is life but a series of inspired follies? The difficulty is to find them to do. Never lose a chance: it doesn't come every day. I shall make a duchess of this draggletailed guttersnipe.

Liza (*strongly deprecating this view of her*). Ah-ah-ah-ow-ow-oo!

Higgins (*carried away*). Yes: in six months—in three if she has a good ear and a quick tongue—I'll take her anywhere and pass her off as anything. We'll start today: now! this moment! Take her away and clean her, Mrs. Pearce. Monkey Brand, if it won't come off any other way. Is there a good fire in the kitchen?

Mrs. Pearce (*protesting*). Yes; but—

Higgins (*storming on*). Take all her clothes off and burn them. Ring up Whiteley or somebody for new ones. Wrap her up in brown paper til they come.

Liza. Youre no gentleman, youre not, to talk of such things. I'm a good girl, I am; and I know what the like of you are, I do.

Higgins. We want none of your Lisson Grove prudery here, young woman. Youve got to learn to behave like a duchess. Take her away, Mrs. Pearce. If she gives you any trouble, wallop her.

Liza (*springing up and running between* Pickering *and* Mrs. Pearce *for protection*). No! I'll call the police, I will.

Mrs. Pearce. But I've no place to put her.

Higgins. Put her in the dustbin.

Liza. Ah-ah-ah-ow-ow-oo!

Pickering. Oh come, Higgins! be reasonable.

Mrs. Pearce (*resolutely*). You must be reasonable, Mr. Higgins: really you must. You can't walk over everybody like this.

Higgins, *thus scolded, subsides. The hurricane is succeeded by a zephyr of amiable surprise.*

Higgins (*with professional exquisiteness of modulation*). *I* walk over everybody! My dear Mrs. Pearce, my dear Pickering, I never had the slightest intention of walking over anyone. All I propose is that we should be kind to this poor girl. We must help her to prepare and fit herself for her new station in life. If I did not express myself clearly it was because I did not wish to hurt her delicacy, or yours.

Liza, *reassured, steals back to her chair.*

Mrs. Pearce (*to* Pickering). Well, did you ever hear anything like that, sir?

Pickering (*laughing heartily*). Never, Mrs. Pearce: never.

Higgins (*patiently*). Whats the matter?

Mrs. Pearce. Well, the matter is, sir, that you can't take a girl up like that as if you were picking up a pebble on the beach.

Higgins. Why not?

Mrs. Pearce. Why not! But you don't know anything about her. What about her parents? She may be married.

Liza. Garn!

Higgins. There! As the girl very properly says, Garn! Married indeed! Don't you know that a woman of that class looks a worn out drudge of fifty a year after she's married?

Liza. Whood marry me?

Higgins (*suddenly resorting to the most thrillingly beautiful low tones in his best elocutionary style*). By George, Eliza, the streets will be strewn with the bodies of men shooting themselves for your sake before I've done with you.

Mrs. Pearce. Nonsense, sir. You mustn't talk like that to her.

Liza (*rising and squaring herself determinedly*). I'm going away. He's off his chump, he is. I don't want no balmies teaching me.

Higgins (*wounded in his tenderest point by her insensibility to his elocution*). Oh, indeed! I'm mad, am I? Very well, Mrs. Pearce; you needn't order the new clothes for her. Throw her out.

Liza (*whimpering*). Nah-ow. You got no right to touch me.

Mrs. Pearce. You see now what comes of being saucy. (*Indicating the door*) This way, please.

Liza (*almost in tears*). I didn't want no clothes. I wouldn't have taken them (*she throws away the handkerchief*). I can buy my own clothes.

Higgins (*deftly retrieving the handkerchief and intercepting her on her reluctant way to the door*). Youre an ungrateful wicked girl. This is my return for offering to take you out of the gutter and dress you beautifully and make a lady of you.

Mrs. Pearce. Stop, Mr. Higgins. I won't allow it. It's you that are wicked. Go home to your parents, girl; and tell them to take better care of you.

Liza. I ain't got no parents. They told me I was big enough to earn my own living and turned me out.

Mrs. Pearce. Wheres your mother?

Liza. I ain't got no mother. Her that turned me out was my sixth stepmother. But I done without them. And I'm a good girl, I am.

Higgins. Very well, then, what on earth is all this fuss about? The girl doesn't belong to anybody—is no use to anybody but me. (*He goes to Mrs. Pearce and begins coaxing*). You can adopt her, Mrs. Pearce: I'm sure a daughter would be a great amusement to you. Now don't make any more fuss. Take her downstairs; and—

Mrs. Pearce. But whats to become of her? Is she to be paid anything? Do be sensible, sir.

Higgins. Oh, pay her whatever is necessary: put it down in the housekeeping book. (*Impatiently*) What on earth will she want with money? She'll have her food and her clothes. She'll only drink if you give her money.

Liza (*turning on him*). Oh you are a brute. It's a lie: nobody ever saw the sign of liquor on me. (*To* Pickering) Oh, sir: youre a gentleman: don't let him speak to me like that.

Pickering (*in good-humored remonstrance*). Does it occur to you, Higgins, that the girl has some feelings?

Higgins (*looking critically at her*). Oh no, I don't think so. Not any feelings that we need bother about. (*Cheerily*) Have you, Eliza?

Liza. I got my feelings same as anyone else.

Higgins (*to* Pickering, *reflectively*). You see the difficulty?

Pickering. Eh? What difficulty?

Higgins. To get her to talk grammar. The mere pronunciation is easy enough.

Liza. I don't want to talk grammar. I wan't to talk like a lady in a flower-shop.

Mrs. Pearce. Will you please keep to the point, Mr. Higgins. I want to know on what terms the girl is to be here. Is she to have any wages? And what is to become of her when youve finished your teaching? You must look ahead a little.

Higgins (*impatiently*). Whats to become of her if I leave her in the gutter? Tell me that, Mrs. Pearce.

Mrs. Pearce. Thats her own business, not yours, Mr. Higgins.

Higgins. Well, when I've done with her, we can throw her back into the gutter; and then it will be her own business again; so thats all right.

Liza. Oh, youve no feeling heart in you: you don't care for nothing but yourself. (*She rises and takes the floor resolutely*). Here! I've had enough of this. I'm going (*making for the door*). You ought to be ashamed of yourself, you ought.

Higgins (*snatching a chocolate cream from the piano, his eyes suddenly beginning to twinkle with mischief*). Have some chocolates, Eliza.

Liza (*halting, tempted*). How do I know what might be in them? I've heard of girls being drugged by the like of you.

Higgins whips out his penknife; cuts a chocolate in two; puts one half into his mouth and bolts it; and offers her the other half.

Higgins. Pledge of good faith. Eliza. I eat one half: you eat the other. (Liza *opens her mouth to retort: he pops the half chocolate into it*). You shall have boxes of them, barrels of them, every day. You shall live on them. Eh?

Liza (*who has disposed of the chocolate after being nearly choked by it*). I wouldn't have ate it, only I'm too ladylike to take it out of my mouth.

Higgins. Listen, Eliza. I think you said you came in a taxi.

Liza. Well, what if I did? I've as good a right to take a taxi as anyone else.

Higgins. You have, Eliza; and in future you shall have as many taxis as you want. You shall go up and down and round the town in a taxi every day. Think of that, Eliza.

Mrs. Pearce. Mr. Higgins: youre tempting the girl. It's not right. She should think of the future.

Higgins. At her age! Nonsense! Time enough to think of the future when you havn't any future to think of. No, Eliza: do as this lady does: think of other people's futures; but never think of your own. Think of chocolates, and taxis, and gold, and diamonds.

Liza. No: I don't want no gold and no diamonds. I'm a good girl, I am. (*She sits down again, with an attempt at dignity.*)

Higgins. You shall remain so, Eliza, under the care of Mrs. Pearce. And you shall marry an officer in the Guards, with a beautiful moustache: the son of a marquis, who will disinherit him for marrying you, but will relent when he sees your beauty and goodness—

Pickering. Excuse me, Higgins; but I really must interfere. Mrs. Pearce is quite right. If this girl is to put herself in your hands for six months for an experiment in teaching, she must understand thoroughly what she's doing.

Higgins. How can she? She's incapable of understanding anything. Besides, do any of us understand what we are doing? If we did, would we ever do it?

Pickering. Very clever, Higgins; but not to the present point. (*To* Eliza) Miss Doolittle—

Liza (*overwhelmed*). Ah-ah-ow-oo!

Higgins. There! Thats all youll get out of Eliza. Ah-ah-ow-oo! No use explaining. As a military man you ought to know that. Give her her orders: thats enough for her. Eliza: you are to live here for the next six months, learning how to speak beautifully, like a lady in a florist's shop. If youre good and do whatever youre told, you shall sleep in a proper bedroom, and have lots to eat, and money to buy chocolates and take rides in taxis. If youre naughty and idle you will sleep in the back kitchen among the black beetles, and be walloped by Mrs. Pearce with a broomstick. At the end of six months you shall go to Buckingham Palace in a carriage, beautifully dressed. If the King finds out youre not a lady, you will be taken by the police to the Tower of London, where your head will be cut off as a warning to other presumptuous flower girls. If you are not found out, you shall have a present of seven-and-sixpence to start life with as a lady in a shop. If you refuse this offer you will be a most ungrateful wicked girl; and the angels will weep for you. (*To* Pickering) Now are you satisfied, Pickering? (*To* Mrs. Pearce) Can I put it more plainly and fairly, Mrs. Pearce?

Mrs. Pearce (*patiently*). I think youd better let me speak to the girl properly in private. I don't know that I can take charge of her or consent to the arrangement at all. Of course I know you don't mean her any harm; but when you get what you call interested in people's accents, you never think or care what may happen to them or you. Come with me, Eliza.

Higgins. Thats all right. Thank you, Mrs. Pearce. Bundle her off to the bathroom.

Liza (*rising reluctantly and suspiciously*). Youre a great bully, you are. I won't stay here if I don't like. I won't let nobody wallop me. I never asked to go to Bucknam Palace. I didnt. I was never in trouble with the police, not me. I'm a good girl—

Mrs. Pearce. Don't answer back, girl. You don't understand the gentleman. Come with me. (*She leads the way to the door, and holds it open for* Eliza.)

Liza (*as she goes out*). Well, what I say is right. I won't go near the King, not if I'm going to have my head cut off. If I'd known what I was letting myself in for, I wouldn't have come here. I always been a good girl; and I never offered to say a word to him; and I don't owe him nothing; and I don't care; and I won't be put upon; and I have my feelings the same as anyone else—

Mrs. Pearce *shuts the door; and* Eliza's *plaints are no longer audible.*

Eliza *is taken upstairs to the third floor greatly to her surprise; for she expected to be taken down to the scullery. There* Mrs. Pearce *opens a door and takes her into a spare bedroom.*

Mrs. Pearce. I will have to put you here. This will be your bedroom.

Liza. O-h, I couldn't sleep here, missus. It's too good for the likes of me. I should be afraid to touch anything. I ain't a duchess yet, you know.

Mrs. Pearce. You have got to make yourself as clean as the room: then you won't be afraid of it. And you must call me Mrs. Pearce, not missus. (*She throws open the door of the dressingroom, now modernized as a bathroom.*)

Liza. Gawd! whats this? Is this where you wash clothes? Funny sort of copper I call it.

Mrs. Pearce. It is not a copper. This is where we wash ourselves, Eliza, and where I am going to wash you.

Liza. You expect me to get into that and wet myself all over! Not me. I should catch my death. I knew a woman did it every Saturday night; and she died of it.

Mrs. Pearce. Mr. Higgins has the gentlemen's bathroom downstairs; and he has a bath every morning, in cold water.

Liza. Ugh! He's made of iron, that man.

Mrs. Pearce. If you are to sit with him and the Colonel and be taught you will have to do the same. They won't like the smell of you if you dont. But you can have the water as hot as you like. There are two taps: hot and cold.

Liza (*weeping*). I couldnt. I dursnt. Its not natural: it would kill me. I've never had a bath in my life: not what youd call a proper one.

Mrs. Pearce. Well, don't you want to be clean and sweet and decent, like a lady? You know you can't be a nice girl inside if youre a dirty slut outside.

Liza. Boohoo!!!!

Mrs. Pearce. Now stop crying and go back into your room and take off all your clothes. Then wrap yourself in this (*taking down a gown from its peg and handing it to her*) and come back to me. I will get the bath ready.

Liza (*all tears*). I cant. I wont. I'm not used to it. I've never took off all my clothes before. It's not right: it's not decent.

Mrs. Pearce. Nonsense, child. Don't you take off all your clothes every night when you go to bed?

Liza (*amazed*). No. Why should I? I should catch my death. Of course I take off my skirt.

Mrs. Pearce. Do you mean that you sleep in the underclothes you wear in the daytime?

Liza. What else have I to sleep in?

Mrs. Pearce. You will never do that again as long as you live here. I will get you a proper nightdress.

Liza. Do you mean change into cold things and lie

awake shivering half the night? You want to kill me, you do.

Mrs. Pearce. I wan't to change you from a frowzy slut to a clean respectable girl fit to sit with the gentlemen in the study. Are you going to trust me and do what I tell you or be thrown out and sent back to your flower basket?

Liza. But you don't know what the cold is to me. You don't know how I dread it.

Mrs. Pearce. Your bed won't be cold here: I will put a hot water bottle in it. (*Pushing her into the bedroom*) Off with you and undress.

Liza. Oh, if only I'd a known what a dreadful thing it is to be clean I'd never have come. I didn't know when I was well off. I—(Mrs. Pearce *pushes her through the door, but leaves it partly open lest her prisoner should take to flight*).

Mrs. Pearce *puts on a pair of white rubber sleeves, and fills the bath, mixing hot and cold, and testing the result with the bath thermometer. She perfumes it with a handful of bath salts and adds a palmful of mustard. She then takes a formidable looking long handled scrubbing brush and soaps it profusely with a ball of scented soap.*

Eliza *comes back with nothing on but the bath gown huddled tightly round her, a piteous spectacle of abject terror.*

Mrs. Pearce. Now come along. Take that thing off.

Liza. Oh I couldnt, Mrs. Pearce: I reely couldnt. I never done such a thing.

Mrs. Pearce. Nonsense. Here: step in and tell me whether it's hot enough for you.

Liza. Ah-oo! Ah-oo! It's too hot.

Mrs. Pearce (*deftly snatching the gown away and throwing* Eliza *down on her back*). It won't hurt you. (*She sets to work with the scrubbing brush.*)

Eliza's *screams are heartrending.*

Meanwhile the Colonel *has been having it out with* Higgins *about* Eliza. Pickering *has come from the hearth to the chair and seated himself astride of it with his arms on the back to cross-examine him.*

Pickering. Excuse the straight question, Higgins. Are you a man of good character where women are concerned?

Higgins (*moodily*). Have you ever met a man of good character where women are concerned?

Pickering. Yes: very frequently.

Higgins (*dogmatically, lifting himself on his hands to the level of the piano, and sitting on it with a bounce*). Well, I havn't. I find that the moment I let a woman make friends with me, she becomes jealous, exacting, suspicious, and a damned nuisance. I find that the moment I let myself make friends with a woman, I become selfish and tyrannical. Women upset everything. When you let them into your life, you find that the woman is driving at one thing and youre driving at another.

Pickering. At what, for example?

Higgins (*coming off the piano restlessly*). Oh, Lord knows! I suppose the woman wants to live her own life; and the man wants to live his; and each tries to drag the other on to the wrong track. One wants to go north and the other south; and the result is that both have to go east, though they both hate the east wind. (*He sits down on the bench at the keyboard.*) So here I am, a confirmed old bachelor, and likely to remain so.

Pickering (*rising and standing over him gravely*). Come, Higgins! You know what I mean. If I'm to be in this business I shall feel responsible for that girl. I hope it's understood that no advantage is to be taken of her position.

Higgins. What! That thing! Sacred, I assure you. (*Rising to explain*) You see, she'll be a pupil; and teaching would be impossible unless pupils were sacred. I've taught scores of American million-airesses how to speak English: the best looking women in the world. I'm seasoned. They might as well be blocks of wood. *I* might as well be a block of wood. It's—

Mrs. Pearce *opens the door. She has* Eliza's *hat in her hand.* Pickering *retires to the easy-chair at the hearth and sits down.*

Higgins (*eagerly*). Well, Mrs. Pearce: is it all right?

Mrs. Pearce (*at the door*). I just wish to trouble you with a word, if I may, Mr. Higgins.

Higgins. Yes, certainly. Come in. (*She comes forward*) Don't burn that, Mrs. Pearce. I'll keep it as a curiosity. (*He takes the hat*).

Mrs. Pearce. Handle it carefully, sir, please. I had to promise her not to burn it; but I had better put it in the oven for a while.

Higgins (*putting it down hastily on the piano*). Oh! thank you. Well, what have you to say to me?

Pickering. Am I in the way?

Mrs. Pearce. Not at all, sir. Mr. Higgins: will you please be very particular what you say before the girl?

Higgins (*sternly*). Of course. I'm always particular

about what I say. Why do you say this to me?

Mrs. Pearce (*unmoved*). No sir: youre not at all particular when youve mislaid anything or when you get a little impatient. Now it doesn't matter before me: I'm used to it. But you really must not swear before the girl.

Higgins (*indignantly*). I swear! (*Most emphatically*) I never swear. I detest the habit. What the devil do you mean?

Mrs. Pearce (*stolidly*). Thats what I mean, sir. You swear a great deal too much. I don't mind your damning and blasting, and what the devil and where the devil and who the devil—

Higgins. Mrs. Pearce: this language from your lips! Really!

Mrs. Pearce (*not to be put off*). —but there is a certain word I must ask you not to use. The girl used it herself when she began to enjoy the bath. It begins with the same letter as bath. She knows no better: she learn't it at her mother's knee. But she must not hear it from your lips.

Higgins (*loftily*). I cannot charge myself with having ever uttered it, Mrs. Pearce. (*She looks at him steadfastly. He adds, hiding an uneasy conscience with a judicial air.*) Except perhaps in a moment of extreme and justifiable excitement.

Mrs. Pearce. Only this morning, sir, you applied it to your boots, to the butter, and to the brown bread.

Higgins. Oh, that! Mere alliteration, Mrs. Pearce, natural to a poet.

Mrs. Pearce. Well, sir, whatever you choose to call it, I beg you not to let the girl hear you repeat it.

Higgins. Oh, very well, very well. Is that all?

Mrs. Pearce. No, sir. We shall have to be very particular with this girl as to personal cleanliness.

Higgins. Certainly. Quite right. Most important.

Mrs. Pearce. I mean not to be slovenly about her dress or untidy in leaving things about.

Higgins (*going to her solemnly*). Just so. I intended to call your attention to that. (*He passes on to* Pickering, *who is enjoying the conversation immensely.*) It is these little things that matter, Pickering. Take care of the pence and the pounds will take care of themselves is as true of personal habits as of money. (*He comes to anchor on the hearthrug, with the air of a man in an unassailable position.*)

Mrs. Pearce. Yes, sir. Then might I ask you not to come down to breakfast in your dressing-gown, or at any rate not to use it as a napkin to the extent you do, sir. And if you would be so good as not to eat everything off the same plate, and to remember not to put the porridge saucepan out of your hand on the clean tablecloth, it would be a better example to the girl. You know you nearly choked yourself with a fishbone in the jam only last week.

Higgins (*routed from the hearthrug and drifting back to the piano*). I may do these things sometimes in absence of mind; but surely I don't do them habitually. (*Angrily*) By the way: my dressing-gown smells most damnably of benzine.

Mrs. Pearce. No doubt it does, Mr. Higgins. But if you will wipe your fingers—

Higgins (*yelling*). Oh very well, very well: I'll wipe them in my hair in future.

Mrs. Pearce. I hope youre not offended, Mr. Higgins.

Higgins (*shocked at finding himself thought capable of an unamiable sentiment*). Not at all, not at all. Youre quite right, Mrs. Pearce: I shall be particularly careful before the girl. Is that all?

Mrs. Pearce. No, sir. Might she use some of those Japanese dresses you brought from abroad? I really can't put her back into her old things.

Higgins. Certainly. Anything you like. Is that all?

Mrs. Pearce. Thank you, sir. Thats all. (*She goes out.*)

Higgins. You know, Pickering, that woman has the most extraordinary ideas about me. Here I am, a shy, diffident sort of man. I've never been able to feel really grown-up and tremendous, like other chaps. And yet she's firmly persuaded that I'm an arbitrary overbearing bossing kind of person. I can't account for it.

Mrs. Pearce *returns.*

Mrs. Pearce. If you please, sir, the trouble's beginning already. Theres a dustman downstairs. Alfred Doolittle, wants to see you. He says you have his daughter here.

Pickering (*rising*). Phew! I say!

Higgins (*promptly*). Send the blackguard up.

Mrs. Pearce. Oh, very well, sir. (*She goes out*).

Pickering. He may not be a blackguard, Higgins.

Higgins. Nonsense. Of course he's a blackguard.

Pickering. Whether he is or not, I'm afraid we shall have some trouble with him.

Higgins (*confidently*). Oh no: I think not. If theres any trouble he shall have it with me, not I with him. And we are sure to get something interesting out of him.

Pickering. About the girl?

Higgins. No. I mean his dialect.

Pickering. Oh!

Mrs. Pearce (*at the door*). Doolittle, sir. (*She admits* Doolittle *and retires.*)

Alfred Doolittle is an elderly but vigorous dustman, clad in the costume of his profession, including a hat with a back brim covering his neck and shoulders. He has well marked and rather interesting features, and seems equally free from fear and conscience. He has a remarkably expressive voice, the result of a habit of giving vent to his feelings without reserve. His present pose is that of wounded honor and stern resolution.

Doolittle (*at the door, uncertain which of the two gentlemen is his man*). Professor Iggins?

Higgins. Here. Good morning. Sit down.

Doolittle. Morning, Governor. (*He sits down magisterially*) I come about a very serious matter, Governor.

Higgins (*to* Pickering). Brought up in Hounslow. Mother Welsh, I should think. (Doolittle *opens his mouth, amazed.* Higgins *continues.*) What do you want, Doolittle?

Doolittle (*menacingly*). I want my daughter: thats what I want. See?

Higgins. Of course you do. Youre her father, arn't you? You don't suppose anyone else wants her, do you? I'm glad to see you have some spark of family feeling left. She's upstairs. Take her away at once.

Doolittle (*rising, fearfully taken aback*). What!

Higgins. Take her away. Do you suppose I'm going to keep your daughter for you?

Doolittle (*remonstrating*). Now, now, look here, Governor. Is this reasonable? Is it fairity to take advantage of a man like this? The girl belongs to me. You got her. Where do I come in? (*He sits down again.*)

Higgins. Your daughter had the audacity to come to my house and ask me to teach her how to speak properly so that she could get a place in a flowershop. This gentleman and my housekeeper have been here all the time. (*Bullying him*) How dare you come here and attempt to blackmail me? You sent her here on purpose.

Doolittle (*protesting*). No, Governor.

Higgins. You must have. How else could you possibly know that she is here?

Doolittle. Don't take a man up like that, Governor.

Higgins. The police shall take you up. This is a plant—a plot to extort money by threats. I shall telephone for the police (*He goes resolutely to the telephone and opens the directory.*)

Doolittle. Have I asked you for a brass farthing? I leave it to the gentleman here: have I said a word about money?

Higgins (*throwing the book aside and marching down on Doolittle with a poser*). What else did you come for?

Doolittle (*sweetly*). Well, what would a man come for? Be human, Governor.

Higgins (*disarmed*). Alfred: did you put her up to it?

Doolittle. So help me, Governor, I never did. I take my Bible oath I ain't seen the girl these two months past.

Higgins. Then how did you know she was here?

Doolittle (*most musical, most melancholy*). I'll tell you, Governor, if youll only let me get a word in. I'm willing to tell you. I'm wanting to tell you. I'm waiting to tell you.

Higgins. Pickering: this chap has a certain natural gift of rhetoric. Observe the rhythm of his native woodnotes wild. "I'm willing to tell you: I'm wanting to tell you: I'm waiting to tell you." Sentimental rhetoric! thats the Welsh strain in him. It also accounts for his mendacity and dishonesty.

Pickering. Oh, please, Higgins: I'm west country myself. (*To* Doolittle) How did you know the girl was here if you didn't send her?

Doolittle. It was like this, Governor. The girl took a boy in the taxi to give him a jaunt. Son of her landlady, he is. He hung about on the chance of her giving him another ride home. Well, she sent him back for her luggage when she heard you was willing for her to stop here. I met the boy at the corner of Long Acre and Endell Street.

Higgins. Public house. Yes?

Doolittle. The poor man's club, Governor: why shouldn't I?

Pickering. Do let him tell his story, Higgins.

Doolittle. He told me what was up. And I ask you, what was my feelings and my duty as a father? I says to the boy, "You bring me the luggage," I says—

Pickering. Why didn't you go for it yourself?

Doolittle. Landlady wouldn't have trusted me with it, Governor. She's that kind of woman: you know. I had to give the boy a penny afore he trusted me with it, the little swine. I brought it to her just to oblige you like, and make myself agreeable. Thats all.

Higgins. How much luggage?

Doolittle. Musical instrument, Governor. A few pictures, a trifle of jewelry, and a bird-cage. She said she didn't want no clothes. What was I to think from that, Governor? I ask you as a parent what was I to think?

Higgins. So you came to rescue her from worse than death eh?

Doolittle (*appreciatively: relieved at being so well understood*). Just so, Governor. Thats right.

Pickering. But why did you bring her luggage if you intended to take her away?

Doolittle. Have I said a word about taking her away? Have I now?

Higgins (*determinedly*). Youre going to take her away, double quick. (*He crosses to the hearth and rings the bell.*)

Doolittle (*rising*). No, Governor. Don't say that. I'm not the man to stand in my girl's light. Heres a career opening for her as you might say; and—

Mrs. Pearce *opens the door and awaits orders.*

Higgins. Mrs. Pearce: this is Eliza's father. He has come to take her away. Give her to him. (*He goes back to the piano, with an air of washing his hands of the whole affair.*)

Doolittle. No. This is a misunderstanding. Listen here—

Mrs. Pearce. He can't take her away, Mr. Higgins: how can he? You told me to burn her clothes.

Doolittle. Thats right. I can't carry the girl through the streets like a blooming monkey, can I? I put it to you.

Higgins. You have put it to me that you want your daughter. Take your daughter. If she has no clothes go out and buy her some.

Doolittle (*desperate*). Wheres the clothes she come in? Did I burn them or did your missus here?

Mrs. Pearce. I am the housekeeper, if you please. I have sent for some clothes for the girl. When they come you can take her away. You can wait in the kitchen. This way, please.

Doolittle, *much troubled, accompanies her to the door; then hesitates: finally turns confidentially to* Higgins.

Doolittle. Listen here, Governor. You and me is men of the world, ain't we?

Higgins. Oh! Men of the world, are we? You'd better go, Mrs. Pearce.

Mrs. Pearce. I think so, indeed, sir. (*She goes, with dignity.*)

Pickering. The floor is yours, Mr. Doolittle.

Doolittle (*to* Pickering). I thank you, Governor. (*To* Higgins, *who takes refuge on the piano bench, a little overwhelmed by the proximity of his visitor; for* Doolittle *has a professional flavor of dust about him.*) Well, the truth is, I've taken a sort of fancy to you, Governor; and if you want the girl, I'm not so set on having her back home again but what I might be open to an arrangement. Regarded in the light of a young woman, she's a fine handsome girl. As a daughter she's not worth her keep; and so I tell you straight. All I ask is my rights as a father; and youre the last man alive to expect me to let her go for nothing; for I can see youre one of the straight sort, Governor. Well, whats a five-pound note to you? and whats Eliza to me? (*He turns to his chair and sits down judicially.*)

Pickering. I think you ought to know, Doolittle, that Mr. Higgins's intentions are entirely honorable.

Doolittle. Course they are, Governor. If I thought they wasn't, I'd ask fifty.

Higgins (*revolted*). Do you mean to say that you would sell your daughter for £50?

Doolittle. Not in a general way I wouldnt; but to oblige a gentleman like you I'd do a good deal, I do assure you.

Pickering. Have you no morals, man?

Doolittle (*unabashed*). Can't afford them, Governor. Neither could you if you was as poor as me. Not that I mean any harm, you know. But if Liza is going to have a bit out of this, why not me too?

Higgins (*troubled*). I don't know what to do, Pickering. There can be no question that as a matter of morals it's a positive crime to give this chap a farthing. And yet I feel a sort of rough justice in his claim.

Doolittle. Thats it, Governor. Thats all I say. A father's heart, as it were.

Pickering. Well, I know the feeling; but really it seems hardly right—

Doolittle. Don't say that, Governor. Don't look at it that way. What am I, Governors both? I ask you, what am I? I'm one of the undeserving poor: thats what I am. Think of what that means to a man. It means that he's up agen middle class morality all the time. If theres anything going, and I put in for a bit of it, it's always the same story: "Youre undeserving; so you can't have it." But my needs is as great as the most deserving widow's that ever got money out of six different charities in one week for the death of the same husband. I don't need less than a deserving man: I need more. I don't eat less hearty than him; and I drink a lot more. I want a bit of amusement, cause I'm a thinking man. I want cheerfulness and a song and a band when I feel low. Well, they charge me just the same for everything as they charge the deserving. What is middle class morality? Just an excuse for never giving me anything. Therefore, I ask you, as two gentlemen, not to play that game on me. I'm playing straight with you. I ain't pretending to be deserving. I'm undeserving; and I mean to go on being undeserving. I like it; and thats the truth. Will you take advantage of a man's nature to do him out of the price of his own daughter what he's brought up and fed and clothed by the sweat of his brow until she's growed big enough to be interesting to you two gentlemen? Is five pounds unreasonable? I put it to you; and I leave it to you.

Higgins (*rising, and going over to* Pickering). Pickering: if we were to take this man in hand for three months, he could choose between a seat in the Cabinet and a popular pulpit in Wales.

Pickering. What do you say to that, Doolittle?

Doolittle. Not me, Governor, thank you kindly. I've heard all the preachers and all the prime ministers—

for I'm a thinking man and game for politics or religion or social reform same as all the other amusements—and I tell you it's a dog's life any way you look at it. Undeserving poverty is my line. Taking one station in society with another, it's—it's—well, it's the only one that has any ginger in it, to my taste.

Higgins. I suppose we must give him a fiver.

Pickering. He'll make a bad use of it, I'm afraid.

Doolittle. Not me, Governor, so help me I wont. Don't you be afraid that I'll save it and spare it and live idle on it. There won't be a penny of it left by Monday: I'll have to go to work same as if I'd never had it. It won't pauperize me, you bet. Just one good spree for myself and the missus, giving pleasure to ourselves and employment to others, and satisfaction to you to think it's not been throwed away. You couldn't spend it better.

Higgins (*taking out his pocket book and coming between Doolittle and the piano*). This is irresistible. Lets give him ten. (*He offers two notes to the dustman.*)

Doolittle. No, Governor. She wouldn't have the heart to spend ten; and perhaps I shouldn't neither. Ten pounds is a lot of money: it makes a man feel prudent like; and then good-bye to happiness. You give me what I ask you, Governor: not a penny more, and not a penny less.

Pickering. Why don't you marry that missus of yours? I rather draw the line at encouraging that sort of immorality.

Doolittle. Tell her so, Governor: tell her so. *I'm* willing. It's me that suffers by it. I've no hold on her. I got to be agreeable to her. I got to give her presents. I got to buy her clothes something sinful. I'm a slave to that woman, Governor, just because I'm not her lawful husband. And she knows it too. Catch her marrying me! Take my advice, Governor—marry Eliza while she's young and don't know no better. If you don't youll be sorry for it after. If you do, she'll be sorry for it after; but better her than you, because youre a man, and she's only a woman and don't know how to be happy anyhow.

Higgins. Pickering: If we listen to this man another minute, we shall have no convictions left. (*To* Doolittle) Five pounds I think you said.

Doolittle. Thank you kindly, Governor.

Higgins. Youre sure you won't take ten?

Doolittle. Not now. Another time, Governor.

Higgins (*handing him a five-pound note*). Here you are.

Doolittle. Thank you, Governor. Good morning. (*He hurries to the door, anxious to get away with his booty. When he opens it he is confronted with a dainty and exquisitely clean young Japanese lady in a simple blue cotton kimono printed cunningly with small white jasmine blossoms.* Mrs. Pearce *is with her. He gets out of her way deferentially and apologizes.*) Beg pardon, miss.

The Japanese Lady. Garn! Don't you know your own daughter?

Doolittle	{ *exclaiming* }	Bly me! it's Eliza!
Higgins	{ *simultaneously* }	Whats that? This!
Pickering		By Jove!

Liza. Don't I look silly?

Higgins. Silly?

Mrs. Pearce (*at the door*). Now, Mr. Higgins, please don't say anything to make the girl conceited about herself.

Higgins (*conscientiously*). Oh! Quite right, Mrs. Pearce. (*To* Eliza) Yes: damned silly.

Mrs. Pearce. Please, sir.

Higgins (*correcting himself*). I mean extremely silly.

Liza. I should look all right with my hat on. (*She takes up her hat; puts it on; and walks across the room to the fireplace with a fashionable air.*)

Higgins. A new fashion, by George! And it ought to look horrible!

Doolittle (*with fatherly pride*). Well, I never thought she'd clean up as good looking as that, Governor. She's a credit to me, ain't she?

Liza. I tell you, it's easy to clean up here. Hot and cold water on tap, just as much as you like, there is. Woolly towels, there is; and a towel horse so hot, it burns your fingers. Soft brushes to scrub yourself, and a wooden bowl of soap smelling like primroses. Now I know why ladies is so clean. Washing's a treat for them. Wish they could see what it is for the like of me!

Higgins. I'm glad the bathroom met with your approval.

Liza. It didnt: not all of it; and I don't care who hears me say it. Mrs. Pearce knows.

Higgins. What was wrong, Mrs. Pearce?

Mrs. Pearce (*blandly*). Oh, nothing, sir. It doesn't matter.

Liza. I had a good mind to break it. I didn't know which way to look. But I hung a towel over it, I did.

Higgins. Over what?

Mrs. Pearce. Over the looking-glass sir.

Higgins. Doolittle: you have brought your daughter up too strictly.

Doolittle. Me! I never brought her up at all, except to give her a lick of a strap now and again. Don't put it on me, Governor. She ain't accustomed to it, you see: thats all. But she'll soon pick up your free-and-easy ways.

Liza. I'm a good girl, I am; and I won't pick up no free-and-easy ways.

Higgins. Eliza: if you say again that youre a good girl, your father shall take you home.

Liza. Not him. You don't know my father. All he come here for was to touch you for some money to get drunk on.

Doolittle. Well, what else would I want money for? To put into the plate in church, I suppose. (*She puts out her tongue at him. He is so incensed by this that* Pickering *presently finds it necessary to step between them.*) Don't you give me none of your lip; and don't let me hear you giving this gentleman any of it neither, or youll hear from me about it. See?

Higgins. Have you any further advice to give her before you go, Doolittle? Your blessing, for instance.

Doolittle. No, Governor: I ain't such a mug as to put up my children to all I know myself. Hard enough to hold them in without that. If you want Eliza's mind improved, Governor, you do it yourself with a strap. So long, gentlemen. (*He turns to go.*)

Higgins (*impressively*). Stop. Youll come regularly to see your daughter. It's your duty, you know. My brother is a clergyman; and he could help you in your talks with her.

Doolittle (*evasively*). Certainly, I'll come, Governor. Not just this week, because I have a job at a distance. But later on you may depend on me. Afternoon, gentlemen. Afternoon, ma'am. (*He touches his hat to* Mrs. Pearce, *who disdains the salutation and goes out. He winks at* Higgins, *thinking him probably a fellow-sufferer from* Mrs. Pearce's *difficult disposition, and follows her.*)

Liza. Don't you believe the old liar. He'd as soon you set a bulldog on him as a clergyman. You won't see him again in a hurry.

Higgins. I don't want to, Eliza. Do you?

Liza. Not me. I don't want never to see him again, I dont. He's a disgrace to me, he is, collecting dust, instead of working at his trade.

Pickering. What is his trade, Eliza?

Liza. Talking money out of other people's pockets into his own. His proper trade's a navvy; and he works at it sometimes too—for exercise—and earns good money at it. Ain't you going to call me Miss Doolittle any more?

Pickering. I beg your pardon, Miss Doolittle. It was a slip of the tongue.

Liza. Oh, I don't mind; only it sounded so genteel. I should just like to take a taxi to the corner of Tottenham Court Road and get out there and tell it to wait for me, just to put the girls in their place a bit. I wouldn't speak to them, you know.

Pickering. Better wait til we get you something really fashionable.

Higgins. Besides, you shouldn't cut your old friends now that you have risen in the world. Thats what we call snobbery.

Liza. You don't call the like of them my friends now, I should hope. Theyve took it out of me often enough with their ridicule when they had the chance; and now I mean to get a bit of my own back. But if I'm to have fashionable clothes, I'll wait. I should like to have some. Mrs. Pearce says youre going to give me some to wear in bed at night different to what I wear in the daytime; but it do seem a waste of money when you could get something to shew. Besides, I never could fancy changing into cold things on a winter night.

Mrs. Pearce (*coming back*). Now, Eliza. The new things have come for you to try on.

Liza. Ah-ow-oo-ooh! (*She rushes out*).

Mrs. Pearce (*following her*). Oh, don't rush about like that, girl. (*She shuts the door behind her.*)

Higgins. Pickering: we have taken on a stiff job.

Pickering (*with conviction*). Higgins: we have.

There seems to be some curiosity as to what Higgins's lessons to Eliza were like. Well, here is a sample: the first one.

Picture Eliza, *in her new clothes, and feeling her inside put out of step by a lunch, dinner, and breakfast of a kind to which it is unaccustomed,* seated with Higgins *and the* Colonel *in the study, feeling like a hospital out-patient at a first encounter with the doctors.*

Higgins, *constitutionally unable to sit still, discomposes her still more by striding restlessly about. But for the reassuring presence and quietude of her friend the* Colonel *she would run for her life, even back to Drury Lane.*

Higgins. Say your alphabet.

Liza. I know my alphabet. Do you think I know nothing? I don't need to be taught like a child.

Higgins (*thundering*). Say your alphabet.

Pickering. Say it, Miss Doolittle. You will understand presently. Do what he tells you; and let him teach you in his own way.

Liza. Oh well, if you put it like that—Ahyee, bəyee, cəyee, dəyee—

Higgins (*with the roar of a wounded lion*). Stop. Listen to this, Pickering. This is what we pay for as elementary education. This unfortunate animal has been locked up for nine years in school at our expense to teach her to speak and read the language of Shakespear and Milton. And the result is Ahyee, Bə-yee, Cə-yee, Də-yee. (*To* Eliza) Say A, B, C, D.

Liza (*almost in tears*). But I'm saying it. Ahyee, Bəyee, Cə-yee—

Higgins. Stop. Say a cup of tea.

Liza. A cappətə-ee.

Higgins. Put your tongue forward until it squeezes against the top of your lower teeth. Now say cup.

Liza. C-c-c—I cant. C-Cup.

Pickering. Good. Splendid, Miss Doolittle.

Higgins. By Jupiter, she's done it at the first shot. Pickering: we shall make a duchess of her. (*To* Eliza) Now do you think you could possibly say tea? Not tə-yee, mind: if you ever say bə-yee cə-yee də-yee again you shall be dragged round the room three times by the hair of your head. (*Fortissimo*) T. T. T. T.

Liza (*weeping*). I can't hear no difference cep that it sounds more genteel-like when you say it.

Higgins. Well, if you can hear that difference, what the devil are you crying for? Pickering: give her a chocolate.

Pickering. No, no. Never mind crying a little, Miss Doolittle: you are doing very well; and the lessons won't hurt. I promise you I won't let him drag you round the room by your hair.

Higgins. Be off with you to Mrs. Pearce and tell her about it. Think about it. Try to do it by yourself: and keep your tongue well forward in your mouth instead of trying to roll it up and swallow it. Another lesson at half-past four this afternoon. Away with you.

Eliza, *still sobbing, rushes from the room.*

And that is the sort of ordeal poor Eliza *has to go through for months before we meet her again on her first appearance in London society of the professional class.*

Act THREE

It is Mrs. Higgins's *at-home day. Nobody has yet arrived. Her drawing room, in a flat on Chelsea Embankment, has three windows looking on the river; and the ceiling is not so lofty as it would be in an older house of the same pretension. The windows are open, giving access to a balcony with flowers in pots. If you stand with your face to the windows, you have the fireplace on your left and the door in the right-hand wall close to the corner nearest the windows.*

Mrs. Higgins *was brought up on Morris and Burne Jones; and her room, which is very unlike her son's room in Wimpole Street, is not crowded with furniture and little tables and nicknacks. In the middle of the room there is a big ottoman; and this, with the carpet, the Morris wallpapers, and the Morris chintz window curtains and brocade covers of the ottoman and its cushions, supply all the ornament, and are much too handsome to be hidden by odds and ends of useless things. A few good oil-paintings from the exhibitions in the Grosvenor Gallery thirty years ago (the Burne Jones, not the Whistler side of them) are on the walls. The only landscape is a Cecil Lawson on the scale of a Rubens. There is a portrait of* Mrs. Higgins *as she was when she defied the fashion in her youth in one of the beautiful Rossettian costumes which, when caricatured by people who did not understand, led to the absurdities of popular estheticism in the eighteen-seventies.*

In the corner diagonally opposite the door Mrs. Higgins, now over sixty and long past taking the trouble to dress out of the fashion, sits writing at an elegantly simple writing-table with a bell button within reach of her hand. There is a Chippendale chair further back in the room between her and the window nearest her side. At the other side of the room, further forward, is an Elizabethan chair roughly carved in the taste of Inigo Jones. On the same side a piano in a decorated case. The corner between the fireplace and the window is occupied by a divan cushioned in Morris chintz.

It is between four and five in the afternoon.

The door is opened violently; and Higgins enters with his hat on.

Mrs. Higgins (*dismayed*). Henry! (*Scolding him*) What are you doing here today? It is my at-home day: you promised not to come. (*As he bends to kiss her, she takes his hat off, and presents it to him.*)

Higgins. Oh bother! (*He throws the hat down on the table.*)

Mrs. Higgins. Go home at once.

Higgins (*kissing her*). I know, mother. I came on purpose.

Mrs. Higgins. But you mustnt. I'm serious, Henry. You offend all my friends: they stop coming whenever they meet you.

Higgins. Nonsense! I know I have no small talk; but people don't mind. (*He sits on the settee.*)

Mrs. Higgins. Oh! don't they? Small talk indeed! What about your large talk? Really, dear, you mustn't stay.

Higgins. I must. I've a job for you. A phonetic job.

Mrs. Higgins. No use, dear. I'm sorry; but I can't get round your vowels; and though I like to get pretty postcards in your patent shorthand, I always have to read the copies in ordinary writing you so thoughtfully send me.

Higgins. Well, this isn't a phonetic job.

Mrs. Higgins. You said it was.

Higgins. Not your part of it. I've picked up a girl.

Mrs. Higgins. Does that mean that some girl has picked you up?

Higgins. Not at all. I don't mean a love affair.

Mrs. Higgins. What a pity!

Higgins. Why?

Mrs. Higgins. Well, you never fall in love with anyone under forty-five. When will you discover that there are some rather nice-looking young women about?

Higgins. Oh, I can't be bothered with young women. My idea of a lovable woman is somebody as like you as possible. I shall never get into the way of seriously liking young women: some habits lie too deep to be changed. (*Rising abruptly and walking about, jingling his money and his keys in his trouser pockets*) Besides, theyre all idiots.

Mrs. Higgins. Do you know what you would do if you really loved me, Henry?

Higgins. Oh bother! What? Marry, I suppose.

Mrs. Higgins. No. Stop fidgeting and take your hands out of your pockets. (*With a gesture of despair, he obeys and sits down again.*) Thats a good boy. Now tell me about the girl.

Higgins. She's coming to see you.

Mrs. Higgins. I don't remember asking her.

Higgins. You didn't. *I* asked her. If youd known her you wouldn't have asked her.

Mrs. Higgins. Indeed! Why?

Higgins. Well, it's like this. She's a common flower girl. I picked her off the kerbstone.

Mrs. Higgins. And invited her to my at-home!

Higgins (*rising and coming to her to coax her*). Oh, thatll be all right. I've taught her to speak properly; and she has strict orders as to her behavior. She's to keep to two subjects: the weather and everybody's health—Fine day and How do you do, you know—and not to let herself go on things in general. That will be safe.

Mrs. Higgins. Safe! To talk about our health! about our insides! perhaps about our outsides! How could you be so silly, Henry?

Higgins (*impatiently*). Well, she must talk about something. (*He controls himself and sits down again.*) Oh, she'll be all right: don't you fuss. Pickering is in it with me. I've a sort of bet on that I'll pass her off as a duchess in six months. I started on her some months ago; and she's getting on like a house on fire. I shall win my bet. She has a quick ear; and she's been easier to teach than my middle-class pupils because she's had to learn a complete new language. She talks English almost as you talk French.

Mrs. Higgins. Thats satisfactory, at all events.

Higgins. Well, it is and it isn't.

Mrs. Higgins. What does that mean?

Higgins. You see, I've got her pronunciation all right; but you have to consider not only how a girl pronounces, but what she pronounces; and thats where—

They are interrupted by the parlormaid, announcing guests.

The Parlormaid. Mrs. and Miss Eynsford Hill. (*She withdraws.*)

Higgins. Oh Lord! (*He rises: snatches his hat from the table; and makes for the door; but before he reaches it his mother introduces him.*)

Mrs. and Miss Eynsford Hill are the mother and daughter who sheltered from the rain in Covent Garden. The mother is well bred, quiet, and has the habitual anxiety of straitened means. The daughter has acquired a gay air of being very much at home in society: the bravado of genteel poverty.

Mrs. Eynsford Hill (*to Mrs. Higgins*). How do you do? (*They shake hands*).

Miss Eynsford Hill. How d'you do? (*She shakes*).

Mrs. Higgins (*introducing*). My son Henry.

Mrs. Eynsford Hill. Your celebrated son! I have so longed to meet you, Professor Higgins.

Higgins (*glumly, making no movement in her direction*). Delighted. (*He backs against the piano and bows brusquely.*)

Miss Eynsford Hill (*going to him with confident familiarity*). How do you do?

Higgins (*staring at her*). I've seen you before somewhere. I havn't the ghost of a notion where; but I've heard your voice. (*Drearily*) It doesn't matter. Youd better sit down.

Mrs. Higgins. I'm sorry to say that my celebrated son has no manners. You mustn't mind him.

Miss Eynsford Hill (*gaily*). I dont. (*She sits in the Elizabethan chair.*)

Mrs. Eynsford Hill (*a little bewildered*). Not at all. (*She sits on the ottoman between her daughter and* Mrs. Higgins, *who has turned her chair away from the writing-table.*)

Higgins. Oh, have I been rude? I didn't mean to be.

He goes to the central window, through which, with his back to the company, he contemplates the river and the flowers in Battersea Park on the opposite bank as if they were a frozen desert.

The parlormaid returns, ushering in Pickering.

The Parlormaid. Colonel Pickering. (*She withdraws.*)

Pickering. How do you do, Mrs. Higgins?

Mrs. Higgins. So glad youve come. Do you know Mrs. Eynsford Hill—Miss Eynsford Hill? (*Exchange of bows. The* Colonel *brings the Chippendale chair a little forward between* Mrs. Hill *and* Mrs. Higgins, *and sits down.*)

Pickering. Has Henry told you what weve come for?

Higgins (*over his shoulder*). We were interrupted: damn it!

Mrs. Higgins. Oh Henry, Henry, really!

Mrs. Eynsford Hill (*half rising*). Are we in the way?

Mrs. Higgins (*rising and making her sit down again*). No, no. You couldn't have come more fortunately: we want you to meet a friend of ours.

Higgins (*turning hopefully*). Yes, by George! We want two or three people. Youll do as well as anybody else.

The parlormaid returns, ushering Freddy.

The Parlormaid. Mr. Eynsford Hill.

Higgins (*almost audibly, past endurance*). God of Heaven! another of them.

Freddy (*shaking hands with* Mrs. Higgins). Ahdedo?

Mrs. Higgins. Very good of you to come. (*Introducing*) Colonel Pickering.

Freddy (*bowing*). Ahdedo?

Mrs. Higgins. I don't think you know my son, Professor Higgins.

Freddy (*going to* Higgins). Ahdedo?

Higgins (*looking at him much as if he were a pickpocket*). I'll take my oath I've met you before somewhere. Where was it?

Freddy. I don't think so.

Higgins (*resignedly*). It don't matter, anyhow. Sit down.

He shakes Freddy's *hand and almost slings him on to the ottoman with his face to the window; then comes round to the other side of it.*

Higgins. Well, here we are, anyhow! (*He sits down on the ottoman next* Mrs. Eynsford Hill, *on her left*). And now, what the devil are we going to talk about until Eliza comes?

Mrs. Higgins. Henry: you are the life and soul of the Royal Society's soirées; but really youre rather trying on more commonplace occasions.

Higgins. Am I? Very sorry. (*Beaming suddenly*) I suppose I am, you know. (*Uproariously*) Ha, ha!

Miss Eynsford Hill (*who considers* Higgins *quite eligible matrimonially*). I sympathize. *I* havn't any small talk. If people would only be frank and say what they really think!

Higgins (*relapsing into gloom*). Lord forbid!

Mrs. Eynsford Hill (*taking up her daughter's cue*). But why?

Higgins. What they think they ought to think is bad enough, Lord knows; but what they really think would break up the whole show. Do you suppose it would be really agreeable if I were to come out now with what *I* really think?

Miss Eynsford Hill (*gaily*). Is it so very cynical?

Higgins. Cynical! Who the dickens said it was cynical? I mean it wouldn't be decent.

Mrs. Eynsford Hill (*seriously*). Oh! I'm sure you don't mean that, Mr. Higgins.

Higgins. You see, we're all savages, more or less. We're supposed to be civilized and cultured—to know all about poetry and philosophy and art and science, and so on; but how many of us know even the meanings of these names? (*To* Miss Hill) What do you know of poetry? (*To* Mrs. Hill) What do you know of science? (*Indicating* Freddy) What does he know of art or science or anything else? What the devil do you imagine I know of philosophy?

Mrs. Higgins (*warningly*). Or of manners, Henry?

The Parlormaid (*opening the door*). Miss Doolittle. (*She withdraws.*)

Higgins (*rising hastily and running to* Mrs. Higgins). Here she is, mother. (*He stands on tiptoe and makes signs over his mother's head to* Eliza *to indicate to her which lady is her hostess.*)

Eliza, *who is exquisitely dressed, produces an impression of such remarkable distinction and beauty as she enters that they all rise, quite fluttered. Guided by* Higgins's *signals, she comes to* Mrs. Higgins *with studied grace.*

Liza (*speaking with pedantic correctness of pronunciation and great beauty of tone*). How do you do, Mrs. Higgins? (*She gasps slightly in making sure of the* H *in* Higgins, *but is quite successful.*) Mr. Higgins told me I might come.

Mrs. Higgins (*cordially*). Quite right: I'm very glad indeed to see you.

Pickering. How do you do, Miss Doolittle?

Liza (*shaking hands with him*). Colonel Pickering, is it not?

Mrs. Eynsford Hill. I feel sure we have met before, Miss Doolittle. I remember your eyes.

Liza. How do you do? (*She sits down on the ottoman gracefully in the place just left vacant by* Higgins.)

Mrs. Eynsford Hill (*introducing*). My daughter Clara.

Liza. How do you do?

Clara (*impulsively*). How do you do? (*She sits down on the ottoman beside* Eliza, *devouring her with her eyes.*)

Freddy (*coming to their side of the ottoman*). I've certainly had the pleasure.

Mrs. Eynsford Hill (*introducing*). My son Freddy.

Liza. How do you do?

Freddy *bows and sits down in the Elizabethan chair, infatuated.*

Higgins (*suddenly*). By George, yes: it all comes back to me! (*They stare at him.*) Covent Garden! (*Lamentably*) What a damned thing!

Mrs. Higgins. Henry, please! (*He is about to sit on the edge of the table*) Don't sit on my writing-table: youll break it.

Higgins (*sulkily*). Sorry.

He goes to the divan, stumbling into the fender and over the fire-irons on his way; extricating himself with muttered imprecations; and finishing his disastrous journey by throwing himself so impatiently on the divan that he almost breaks it. Mrs. Higgins *looks at him, but controls herself and says nothing.*

A long and painful pause ensues.

Mrs. Higgins (*at last, conversationally*). Will it rain, do you think?

Liza. The shallow depression in the west of these islands is likely to move slowly in an easterly direction. There are no indications of any great change in the barometrical situation.

Freddy. Ha! ha! how awfully funny!

Liza. What is wrong with that, young man? I bet I got it right.

Freddy. Killing!

Mrs. Eynsford Hill. I'm sure I hope it won't turn cold. Theres so much influenza about. It runs right through our whole family regularly every spring.

Liza (*darkly*). My aunt died of influenza: so they said.

Mrs. Eynsford Hill. (*clicks her tongue sympathetically*)!!!

Liza (*in the same tragic tone*). But it's my belief they done the old woman in.

Mrs. Higgins (*puzzled*). Done her in?

Liza. Y-e-e-e-es, Lord love you! Why should she die of

influenza? She come through diphtheria right enough the year before. I saw her with my own eyes. Fairly blue with it, she was. They all thought she was dead; but my father he kept ladling gin down her throat til she came to so sudden that she bit the bowl off the spoon.

Mrs. Eynsford Hill (*startled*). Dear me!

Liza (*piling up the indictment*). What call would a woman with that strength in her have to die of influenza? What become of her new straw hat that should have come to me? Somebody pinched it; and what I say is, them as pinched it done her in.

Mrs. Eynsford Hill. What does doing her in mean?

Higgins (*hastily*). Oh, thats the new small talk. To do a person in means to kill them.

Mrs. Eynsford Hill (*to* Eliza, *horrified*). You surely don't believe that your aunt was killed?

Liza. Do I not! Them she lived with would have killed her for a hat-pin, let alone a hat.

Mrs. Eynsford Hill. But it can't have been right for your father to pour spirits down her throat like that. It might have killed her.

Liza. Not her. Gin was mother's milk to her. Besides, he'd poured so much down his own throat that he knew the good of it.

Mrs. Eynsford Hill. Do you mean that he drank?

Liza. Drank! My word! Something chronic.

Mrs. Eynsford Hill. How dreadful for you!

Liza. Not a bit. It never did him no harm what I could see. But then he did not keep it up regular. (*Cheerfully*) On the burst, as you might say, from time to time. And always more agreeable when he had a drop in. When he was out of work, my mother used to give him fourpence and tell him to go out and not come back until he'd drunk himself cheerful and loving-like. Theres lots of women has to make their husbands drunk to make them fit to live with. (*Now quite at her ease*) You see, it's like this. If a man has a bit of a conscience, it always takes him when he's sober; and then it makes him low-spirited. A drop of booze just takes that off and makes him happy. (*To* Freddy, *who is in convulsions of suppressed laughter*) Here! what are you sniggering at?

Freddy. The new small talk. You do it so awfully well.

Liza. If I was doing it proper, what was you laughing at? (*To* Higgins) Have I said anything I oughtnt?

Mrs. Higgins (*interposing*). Not at all, Miss Doolittle.

Liza. Well, thats a mercy, anyhow. (*Expansively*) What I always say is—

Higgins (*rising and looking at his watch*). Ahem!

Liza (*looking round at him; taking the hint; and rising*). Well: I must go. (*They all rise.* Freddy *goes to the door.*) So pleased to have met you. Goodbye. (*She shakes hands with* Mrs. Higgins.)

Mrs. Higgins. Goodbye.

Liza. Goodbye, Colonel Pickering.

Pickering. Goodbye, Miss Doolittle. (*They shake hands.*)

Liza (*nodding to the others*). Goodbye, all.

Freddy (*opening the door for her*). Are you walking across the Park, Miss Doolittle? If so—

Liza (*perfectly elegant diction*). Walk! Not bloody likely. (*Sensation*). I am going in a taxi. (*She goes out.*)

Pickering *gasps and sits down.* Freddy *goes out on the balcony to catch another glimpse of* Eliza.

Mrs. Eynsford Hill (*suffering from shock*). Well, I really can't get used to the new ways.

Clara (*throwing herself discontentedly into the Elizabethan chair*). Oh, it's all right, mamma, quite right. People will think we never go anywhere or see anybody if you are so old-fashioned.

Mrs. Eynsford Hill. I daresay I am very old-fashioned; but I do hope you won't begin using that expression, Clara. I have got accustomed to hear you talking about men as rotters, and calling everything filthy and beastly; though I do think it horrible and unladylike. But this last is really too much. Don't you think so, Colonel Pickering?

Pickering. Don't ask me. I've been away in India for several years; and manners have changed so much that I sometimes don't know whether I'm at a respectable dinner-table or in a ship's forecastle.

Clara. It's all a matter of habit. Theres no right or wrong in it. Nobody means anything by it. And it's so quaint, and gives such a smart emphasis to things that are not in themselves very witty. I find the new small talk delightful and quite innocent.

Mrs. Eynsford Hill (*rising*). Well, after that, I think it's time for us to go.

Pickering *and* Higgins *rise.*

Clara (*rising*). Oh yes: we have three at-homes to go to still. Goodbye, Mrs. Higgins. Goodbye, Colonel Pickering. Goodbye, Professor Higgins.

Higgins (*coming grimly at her from the divan, and accompanying her to the door*). Goodbye. Be sure you try on that small talk at the three at-homes. Don't be nervous about it. Pitch it in strong.

Clara (*all smiles*). I will. Goodbye. Such nonsense, all this early Victorian prudery!

Higgins (*tempting her*). Such damned nonsense!

Clara. Such bloody nonsense!

Mrs. Eynsford Hill (*convulsively*). Clara!

Clara. Ha! ha! (*She goes out radiant, conscious of being thoroughly up to date, and is heard descending the stairs in a stream of silvery laughter.*)

Freddy (*to the heavens at large*). Well, I ask you—(*He gives it up, and comes to* Mrs. Higgins.) Goodbye.

Mrs. Higgins (*shaking hands*). Goodbye. Would you like to meet Miss Doolittle again?

Freddy (*eagerly*). Yes, I should, most awfully.

Mrs. Higgins. Well, you know my days.

Freddy. Yes. Thanks awfully. Goodbye. (*He goes out.*)

Mrs. Eynsford Hill. Goodbye, Mr. Higgins.

Higgins. Goodbye. Goodbye.

Mrs. Eynsford Hill (*to* Pickering). It's no use. I shall never be able to bring myself to use that word.

Pickering. Dont. It's not compulsory, you know. Youll get on quite well without it.

Mrs. Eynsford Hill. Only, Clara is so down on me if I am not positively reeking with the latest slang. Goodbye.

Pickering. Goodbye. (*They shake hands.*)

Mrs. Eynsford Hill (*to* Mrs. Higgins). You mustn't mind Clara. (Pickering, *catching from her lowered tone that this is not meant for him to hear, discreetly joins Higgins at the window.*) We're so poor! and she gets so few parties, poor child! She doesn't quite know. (Mrs. Higgins, *seeing that her eyes are moist, takes her hand sympathetically and goes with her to the door.*) But the boy is nice. Don't you think so?

Mrs. Higgins. Oh, quite nice. I shall always be delighted to see him.

Mrs. Eynsford Hill. Thank you, dear. Goodbye. (*She goes out.*)

Higgins (*eagerly*). Well? Is Eliza presentable? (*he swoops on his mother and drags her to the ottoman, where she sits down in Eliza's place with her son on her left.*)

Pickering *returns to his chair on her right.*

Mrs. Higgins. You silly boy, of course she's not presentable. She's a triumph of your art and of her dressmaker's; but if you suppose for a moment that she doesn't give herself away in every sentence she utters, you must be perfectly cracked about her.

Pickering. But don't you think something might be done? I mean something to eliminate the sanguinary element from her conversation.

Mrs. Higgins. Not as long as she is in Henry's hands.

Higgins (*aggrieved*). Do you mean that my language is improper?

Mrs. Higgins. No, dearest: it would be quite proper— say on a canal barge; but it would not be proper for her at a garden party.

Higgins (*deeply injured*). Well I must say—

Pickering (*interrupting him*). Come, Higgins: you must learn to know yourself. I havn't heard such language as yours since we used to review the volunteers in Hyde Park twenty years ago.

Higgins (*sulkily*). Oh, well, if you say so, I suppose I don't always talk like a bishop.

Mrs. Higgins (*quieting Henry with a touch*). Colonel Pickering: will you tell me what is the exact state of things in Wimpole Street?

Pickering (*cheerfully: as if this completely changed the subject*). Well, I have come to live there with Henry. We work together at my Indian Dialects; and we think it more convenient—

Mrs. Higgins. Quite so. I know all about that: it's an excellent arrangement. But where does this girl live?

Higgins. With us, of course. Where should she live?

Mrs. Higgins. But on what terms? Is she a servant? If not, what is she?

Pickering (*slowly*). I think I know what you mean, Mrs. Higgins.

Higgins. Well, dash me if *I* do! I've had to work at the girl every day for months to get her to her present pitch. Besides, she's useful. She knows where my things are, and remembers my appointments and so forth.

Mrs. Higgins. How does your housekeeper get on with her?

Higgins. Mrs. Pearce? Oh, she's jolly glad to get so much taken off her hands; for before Eliza came, she used to have to find things and remind me of my appointments. But she's got some silly bee in her bonnet about Eliza. She keeps saying "You don't think, sir": doesn't she, Pick?

Pickering. Yes: thats the formula. "You don't think, sir." Thats the end of every conversation about Eliza.

Higgins. As if I ever stop thinking about the girl and her confounded vowels and consonants. I'm worn out, thinking about her, and watching her lips and her teeth and her tongue, not to mention her soul, which is the quaintest of the lot.

Mrs. Higgins. You certainly are a pretty pair of babies, playing with your live doll.

Higgins. Playing! The hardest job I ever tackled: make no mistake about that, mother. But you have no idea how frightfully interesting it is to take a human being and change her into a quite different human being by creating a new speech for her. It's filling up the deepest gulf that separates class from class and soul from soul.

Pickering (*drawing his chair closer to* Mrs. Higgins *and bending over to her eagerly*). Yes: it's enormously interesting. I assure you, Mrs. Higgins, we take Eliza very seriously. Every week—every day almost—there is some new change. (*Closer again*) We keep records of every stage—dozens of gramophone disks and photographs—

Higgins (*assailing her at the other ear*). Yes, by George: it's the most absorbing experiment I ever tackled. She regularly fills our lives up: doesn't she, Pick?

Pickering. We're always talking Eliza.

Higgins. Teaching Eliza.

Pickering. Dressing Eliza.

Mrs. Higgins. What!

Higgins. Inventing new Elizas.

Higgins.
Pickering. *[speaking together]*

> You know, she has the most extra-
>   ordinary quickness of ear:
> I assure you, my dear Mrs Higgins
>   that girl

Higgins.
Pickering.

> just like a parrot. Ive tried her with
>   every
> is a genius. She can play the piano
>   quite beautifully.

Higgins.
Pickering.

> possible sort of sound that a human
>   being can make—
> We have taken her to classical con-
>   certs and to music

Higgins.
Pickering.

> Continental dialects, African dialects,
>   Hottentot
> halls; and it's all the same to her: she
>   plays everything

Higgins.
Pickering.

> clicks, things it took me years to get
>   hold of; and
> she hears right off when she comes
>   home, whether it's

Higgins.
Pickering.

> she picks them up like a shot, right
>   away, as if she had
> Beethoven and Brahms or Lehar and
>   Lionel Monckton;

Higgins.
Pickering.

> been at it all her life.
> though six months ago, she'd never as
>   much as touched a piano—

Mrs. Higgins (*putting her fingers in her ears, as they are by this time shouting one another down with an intolerable noise*). Sh-sh-sh—sh!

(*They stop.*)

Pickering. I beg your pardon. (*He draws his chair back apologetically.*)

Higgins. Sorry. When Pickering starts shouting nobody can get a word in edgeways.

Mrs. Higgins. Be quiet, Henry. Colonel Pickering: don't you realize that when Eliza walked into Wimpole Street, something walked in with her?

Pickering. Her father did. But Henry soon got rid of him.

Mrs. Higgins. It would have been more to the point if her mother had. But as her mother didn't something else did.

Pickering. But what?

Mrs. Higgins (*unconsciously dating herself by the word*). A problem.

Pickering. Oh I see. The problem of how to pass her off as a lady.

Higgins. I'll solve that problem. I've half solved it already.

Mrs. Higgins. No, you two infinitely stupid male creatures: the problem of what is to be done with her afterwards.

Higgins. I don't see anything in that. She can go her own way, with all the advantages I have given her.

Mrs. Higgins. The advantages of that poor woman who was here just now! The manners and habits that disqualify a fine lady from earning her own living without giving her a fine lady's income! Is that what you mean?

Pickering (*indulgently, being rather bored*). Oh, that will be all right, Mrs. Higgins. (*He rises to go.*)

Higgins (*rising also*). We'll find her some light employment.

Pickering. She's happy enough. Don't you worry about her. Goodbye. (*He shakes hands as if he were consoling a frightened child, and makes for the door.*)

Higgins. Anyhow, theres no good bothering now. The thing's done. Goodbye, mother. (*He kisses her, and follows* Pickering.)

Pickering (*turning for a final consolation*). There are plenty of openings. We'll do whats right. Goodbye.

Higgins (*to* Pickering *as they go out together*). Lets take her to the Shakespear exhibition at Earls Court.

Pickering. Yes: lets. Her remarks will be delicious.

Higgins. She'll mimic all the people for us when we get home.

Pickering. Ripping. (*Both are heard laughing as they go downstairs.*)

Mrs. Higgins (*rises with an impatient bounce, and returns to her work at the writing-table. She sweeps a litter of disarranged papers out of the way; snatches a sheet of paper from her stationery case; and tries resolutely to write. At the third time she gives it up; flings down her pen; grips the table angrily and exclaims*). Oh, men! men!! men!!!

Clearly Eliza *will not pass as a duchess yet; and* Higgins's *bet remains unwon. But the six months are not yet exhausted; and just in time* Eliza *does actually pass as a princess. For a glimpse of how she did it imagine an Embassy in London one summer evening after dark. The hall door has an awning and a carpet across the sidewalk to the kerb, because a grand reception is in progress. A small crowd is lined up to see the guests arrive.*

A Rolls-Royce car drives up. Pickering *in evening dress, with medals and orders, alights, and hands out* Eliza, *in opera cloak, evening dress, diamonds, fan, flowers and all accessories.* Higgins *follows. The car drives off; and the three go up the steps and into the house, the door opening for them as they approach.*

Inside the house they find themselves in a spacious hall from which the grand staircase rises. On the left are the arrangements for the gentlemen's cloaks. The male guests are depositing their hats and wraps there.

On the right is a door leading to the ladies' cloakroom. Ladies are going in cloaked and coming out in splendor. Pickering *whispers to* Eliza *and points out the ladies' room. She goes into it.* Higgins *and* Pickering *take off their overcoats and take tickets for them from the attendant.*

One of the guests, occupied in the same way, has his back turned. Having taken his ticket, he turns round and reveals himself as an important looking young man with an astonishingly hairy face. He has an enormous moustache, flowing out into luxuriant whiskers. Waves of hair cluster on his brow. His hair is cropped closely at the back, and glows with oil. Otherwise he is very smart. He wears several worthless orders. He is evidently a foreigner, guessable as a whiskered Pandour from Hungary; but in spite of the ferocity of his moustache he is amiable and genially voluble.

Recognizing Higgins, *he flings his arms wide apart and approaches him enthusiastically.*

Whiskers. Maestro, maestro (*he embraces* Higgins *and kisses him on both cheeks*). You remember me?

Higgins. No I don't. Who the devil are you?

Whiskers. I am your pupil: your first pupil, your best and greatest pupil. I am little Nepommuck, the marvellous boy. I have made your name famous throughout Europe. You teach me phonetic. You cannot forget ME.

Higgins. Why don't you shave?

Nepommuck. I have not your imposing appearance, your chin, your brow. Nobody notices me when I shave. Now I am famous: they call me Hairy Faced Dick.

Higgins. And what are you doing here among all these swells?

Nepommuck. I am interpreter. I speak 32 languages. I am indispensable at these international parties. You are great cockney specialist: you place a man anywhere in London the moment he open his mouth. I place any man in Europe.

A footman hurries down the grand staircase and comes to Nepommuck.

Footman. You are wanted upstairs. Her Excellency cannot understand the Greek gentleman.

Nepommuck. Thank you, yes, immediately.

The footman goes and is lost in the crowd.

Nepommuck (*to* Higgins). This Greek diplomatist pretends he cannot speak nor understand English. He cannot deceive me. He is the son of a Clerkenwell watchmaker. He speaks English so villainously that he dare not utter a word of it without betraying his origin. I help him to pretend; but I make him pay through the nose. I make them all pay. Ha ha! (*He hurries upstairs.*)

Pickering. Is this fellow really an expert? Can he find out Eliza and blackmail her?

Higgins. We shall see. If he finds her out I lose my bet.

Eliza *comes from the cloakroom and joins them.*

Pickering. Well, Eliza, now for it. Are you ready?

Liza. Are you nervous, Colonel?

Pickering. Frightfully. I feel exactly as I felt before my first battle. It's the first time that frightens.

Liza. It is not the first time for me, Colonel. I have done this fifty times—hundreds of times—in my little piggery in Angel Court in my day-dreams. I am in a dream now. Promise me not to let Professor Higgins wake me; for if he does I shall forget everything and talk as I used to in Drury Lane.

Pickering. Not a word, Higgins. (*To* Eliza) Now ready?

Liza. Ready.

Pickering. Go.

They mount the stairs, Higgins *last.* Pickering *whispers to the footman on the first landing.*

First Landing Footman. Miss Doolittle, Colonel Pickering, Professor Higgins.

Second Landing Footman. Miss Doolittle, Colonel Pickering, Professor Higgins.

At the top of the staircase the Ambassador *and his wife, with* Nepommuck *at her elbow, are receiving.*

Hostess (*taking* Eliza's *hand*). How d'ye do?

Host (*same play*). How d'ye do? How d'ye do, Pickering?

Liza (*with a beautiful gravity that awes her hostess*). How do you do? (*She passes on to the drawing room.*)

Hostess. Is that your adopted daughter, Colonel Pickering? She will make a sensation.

Pickering. Most kind of you to invite her for me. (*He passes on.*)

Hostess (*to* Nepommuck). Find out all about her.

Nepommuck (*bowing*). Excellency—(*he goes into the crowd*).

Host. How d'ye do, Higgins? You have a rival here tonight. He introduced himself as your pupil. Is he any good?

Higgins. He can learn a language in a fortnight—knows dozens of them. A sure mark of a fool. As a phonetician, no good whatever.

Hostess. How d'ye do, Professor?

Higgins. How do you do? Fearful bore for you this sort of thing. Forgive my part in it. (*He passes on.*)

In the drawing room and its suite of salons the reception is in full swing. Eliza passes through. She is so intent on her ordeal that she walks like a somnambulist in a desert instead of a débutante in a fashionable crowd. They stop talking to look at her, admiring her dress, her jewels, and her strangely attractive self. Some of the younger ones at the back stand on their chairs to see.

The Host *and* Hostess *come in from the staircase and mingle with their guests.* Higgins, *gloomy and contemptuous of the whole business, comes into the group where they are chatting.*

Hostess. Ah, here is Professor Higgins: he will tell us. Tell us all about the wonderful young lady, Professor.

Higgins (*almost morosely*). What wonderful young lady?

Hostess. You know very well. They tell me there has been nothing like her in London since people stood on their chairs to look at Mrs. Langtry.

Nepommuck *joins the group, full of news.*

Hostess. Ah, here you are at last, Nepommuck. Have you found out all about the Doolittle lady?

Nepommuck. I have found out all about her. She is a fraud.

Hostess. A fraud! Oh no.

Nepommuck. YES, yes. She cannot deceive me. Her name cannot be Doolittle.

Higgins. Why?

Nepommuck. Because Doolittle is an English name. And she is not English.

Hostess. Oh, nonsense! She speaks English perfectly.

Nepommuck. Too perfectly. Can you shew me any English woman who speaks English as it should be spoken? Only foreigners who have been taught to speak it speak it well.

Hostess. Certainly she terrified me by the way she said How d'ye do. I had a schoolmistress who talked like that; and I was mortally afraid of her. But if she is not English what is she?

Nepommuck. Hungarian.

All the Rest. Hungarian!

Nepommuck. Hungarian. And of royal blood. I am Hungarian. My blood is royal.

Higgins. Did you speak to her in Hungarian?

Nepommuck. I did. She was very clever. She said "Please speak to me in English: I do not understand French." French! She pretends not to know the difference between Hungarian and French. Impossible: she knows both.

Higgins. And the blood royal? How did you find that out?

Nepommuck. Instinct, maestro, instinct. Only the Magyar races can produce that air of the divine right, those resolute eyes. She is a princess.

Host. What do you say, Professor?

Higgins. I say an ordinary London girl out of the gutter and taught to speak by an expert. I place her in Drury Lane.

Nepommuck. Ha ha ha! Oh, maestro, maestro, you are mad on the subject of cockney dialects. The London gutter is the whole world for you.

Higgins (*to the* Hostess). What does your Excellency say?

Hostess. Oh, of course I agree with Nepommuck. She must be a princess at least.

Host. Not necessarily legitimate, of course. Morganatic perhaps. But that is undoubtedly her class.

Higgins. I stick to my opinion.

Hostess. Oh, you are incorrigible.

The group breaks up, leaving Higgins *isolated.* Pickering *joins him.*

Pickering. Where is Eliza? We must keep an eye on her.

Eliza joins them.

Liza. I don't think I can bear much more. The people all stare so at me. An old lady has just told me that I speak exactly like Queen Victoria. I am sorry if I have lost your bet. I have done my best; but nothing can make me the same as these people.

Pickering. You have not lost it, my dear. You have won it ten times over.

Higgins. Let us get out of this. I have had enough of chattering to these fools.

Pickering. Eliza is tired; and I am hungry. Let us clear out and have supper somewhere.

FOUR

The Wimpole Street laboratory. Midnight. Nobody in the room. The clock on the mantelpiece strikes twelve. The fire is not alight: it is a summer night.

Presently Higgins *and* Pickering *are heard on the stairs.*

Higgins (*calling down to* Pickering). I say, Pick: lock up, will you? I shan't be going out again.

Pickering. Right. Can Mrs. Pearce go to bed? We don't want anything more, do we?

Higgins. Lord, no!

Eliza *opens the door and is seen on the lighted landing in all the finery in which she has just won* Higgins's *bet for him. She comes to the hearth, and switches on the electric lights there. She is tired: her pallor contrasts strongly with her dark eyes and hair; and her expression is almost tragic. She takes off her cloak; puts her fan and gloves on the piano; and sits down on the bench, brooding and silent.* Higgins, *in evening dress, with overcoat and hat, comes in, carrying a smoking jacket which he has picked up downstairs. He takes off the hat and overcoat; throws them carelessly on the newspaper stand; disposes of his coat in the same way; puts on the smoking jacket; and throws himself wearily into the easy-chair at the hearth.* Pickering, *similarly attired, comes in. He also takes off his hat and overcoat, and is about to throw them on* Higgins's *when he hesitates.*

Pickering. I say: Mrs. Pearce will row if we leave these things lying about in the drawing room.

Higgins. Oh, chuck them over the bannisters into the hall. She'll find them there in the morning and put them away all right. She'll think we were drunk.

Pickering. We are, slightly. Are there any letters?

Higgins. I didn't look. (Pickering *takes the overcoats and hats and goes downstairs. Higgins begins half singing half yawning an air from La Fanciulla del Golden West. Suddenly he stops and exclaims*) I wonder where the devil my slippers are!

Eliza *looks at him darkly; then rises suddenly and leaves the room.*

Higgins *yawns again, and resumes his song.*

Pickering *returns, with the contents of the letterbox in his hand.*

Pickering. Only circulars, and this coroneted billet-doux for you. (*He throws the circulars into the fender, and posts himself on the hearthrug, with his back to the grate.*)

Higgins (*glancing at the billet-doux*). Money-lender. (*He throws the letter after the circulars.*)

Eliza *returns with a pair of large down-at-heel slippers. She places them on the carpet before* Higgins, *and sits as before without a word.*

Higgins (*yawning again*). Oh Lord! What an evening! What a crew! What a silly tomfoolery! (*He raises his shoe to unlace it, and catches sight of the slippers. He stops unlacing and looks at them as if they had appeared there of their own accord.*) Oh! theyre there, are they?

Pickering (*stretching himself*). Well, I feel a bit tired. It's been a long day. The garden party, a dinner party, and the reception! Rather too much of a good thing. But youve won your bet, Higgins. Eliza did the trick, and something to spare, eh?

Higgins (*fervently*). Thank God it's over!

Eliza *flinches violently; but they take no notice of her; and she recovers herself and sits stonily as before.*

Pickering. Were you nervous at the garden party? *I* was. Eliza didn't seem a bit nervous.

Higgins. Oh, she wasn't nervous. I knew she'd be all right. No: it's the strain of putting the job through all these months that has told on me. It was interesting enough at first, while we were at the phonetics; but after that I got deadly sick of it. If I hadn't backed myself to do it I should have chucked the whole thing up two months ago. It was a silly notion: the whole thing has been a bore.

Pickering. Oh come! the garden party was frightfully exciting. My heart began beating like anything.

Higgins. Yes, for the first three minutes. But when I saw we were going to win hands down, I felt like a bear in a cage, hanging about doing nothing. The dinner was worse: sitting gorging there for over an hour, with nobody but a damned fool of a fashionable woman to talk to! I tell you, Pickering, never again for me. No more artificial duchesses. The whole thing has been simple purgatory.

Pickering. Youve never been broken in properly to the social routine. (*Strolling over to the piano*) I rather enjoy dipping into it occasionally myself: it makes me feel young again. Anyhow, it was a great success: an immense success. I was quite frightened once or twice because Eliza was doing it so well. You see, lots of the real people can't do it at all: theyre such fools that they think style comes by nature to people in their position; and so they never learn. Theres always something professional about doing a thing superlatively well.

Higgins. Yes: thats what drives me mad: the silly people don't know their own silly business. (*Rising*) However, it's over and done with; and now I can go to bed at last without dreading tomorrow.

Eliza's *beauty becomes murderous.*

Pickering. I think I shall turn in too. Still, it's been a great occasion: a triumph for you. Goodnight. (*He goes.*)

Higgins (*following him*). Goodnight. (*Over his shoulder, at the door*) Put out the lights, Eliza; and tell Mrs. Pearce not to make coffee for me in the morning: I'll take tea. (*He goes out.*)

Eliza *tries to control herself and feel indifferent as she rises and walks across to the hearth to switch off the lights. By the time she gets there she is on the point of screaming. She sits down in Higgins's chair and holds on hard to the arms. Finally she gives way and flings herself furiously on the floor, raging.*

Higgins (*in despairing wrath outside*). What the devil have I done with my slippers? (*He appears at the door.*)

Liza (*snatching up the slippers, and hurling them at him one after the other with all her force*). There are your slippers. And there. Take your slippers; and may you never have a day's luck with them!

Higgins (*astounded*). What on earth—! (*He comes to her.*) Whats the matter? Get up. (*He pulls her up.*) Anything wrong?

Liza (*breathless*) Nothing wrong—with you. I've won your bet for you, havn't I? Thats enough for you. *I* don't matter, I suppose.

Higgins. You won my bet! You! Presumptuous insect!

I won it. What did you throw those slippers at me for?

Liza. Because I wanted to smash your face. I'd like to kill you, you selfish brute. Why didn't you leave me where you picked me out of—in the gutter? You thank God it's all over, and that now you can throw me back again there, do you? (*She crisps her fingers frantically.*)

Higgins (*looking at her in cool wonder*). The creature is nervous, after all.

Liza. (*gives a suffocated scream of fury, and instinctively darts her nails at his face*)!!

Higgins (*catching her wrists*). Ah! would you? Claws in, you cat. How dare you shew your temper to me? Sit down and be quiet. (*He throws her roughly into the easy-chair.*)

Liza (*crushed by superior strength and weight*). Whats to become of me? Whats to become of me?

Higgins. How the devil do I know whats to become of you? What does it matter what becomes of you?

Liza. You don't care. I know you don't care. You wouldn't care if I was dead. I'm nothing to you— not so much as them slippers.

Higgins (*thundering*). Those slippers.

Liza (*with bitter submission*). Those slippers. I didn't think it made any difference now.

A pause, Eliza *hopeless and crushed.* Higgins *a little uneasy.*

Higgins (*in his loftiest manner*). Why have you begun going on like this? May I ask whether you complain of your treatment here?

Liza. No.

Higgins. Has anybody behaved badly to you? Colonel Pickering? Mrs. Pearce? Any of the servants?

Liza. No.

Higgins. I presume you don't pretend that *I* have treated you badly?

Liza. No.

Higgins. I am glad to hear it. (*He moderates his tone.*) Perhaps youre tired after the strain of the day. Will you have a glass of champagne? (*He moves towards the door.*)

Liza. No. (*Recollecting her manners*) Thank you.

Higgins (*good-humored again*). This has been coming on you for some days. I suppose it was natural for you to be anxious about the garden party. But thats all over now. (*He pats her kindly on the shoulder. She writhes.*) Theres nothing more to worry about.

Liza. No. Nothing more for you to worry about. (*She suddenly rises and gets away from him by going to the piano bench, where she sits and hides her face.*) Oh God! I wish I was dead.

Higgins (*staring after her in sincere surprise*). Why? In heaven's name, why? (*Reasonably, going to her*) Listen to me, Eliza. All this irritation is purely subjective.

Liza. I don't understand. I'm too ignorant.

Higgins. It's only imagination. Low spirits and nothing else. Nobody's hurting you. Nothing's wrong. You go to bed like a good girl and sleep it off. Have a little cry and say your prayers: that will make you comfortable.

Liza. I heard your prayers. "Thank God it's all over!"

Higgins (*impatiently*). Well, don't you thank God it's all over? Now you are free and can do what you like.

Liza (*pulling herself together in desperation*). What am I fit for? What have you left me fit for? Where am I to go? What am I to do? Whats to become of me?

Higgins (*enlightened, but not at all impressed*). Oh, thats whats worrying you, is it? (*He thrusts his hands into his pockets, and walks about in his usual manner, rattling the contents of his pockets, as if condescending to a trivial subject out of pure kindness.*) I shouldn't bother about it if I were you. I should imagine you won't have much difficulty in settling yourself somewhere or other, though I hadn't quite realized that you were going away. (*She looks quickly at him: he does not look at her, but examines the dessert stand on the piano and decides that he will eat an apple.*) You might marry, you know. (*He bites a large piece out of the apple and munches it noisily.*) You see, Eliza, all men are not confirmed old bachelors like me and the Colonel. Most men are the marrying sort (poor devils!); and youre not bad-looking: it's quite a pleasure to look at you sometimes—not now, of course, because youre crying and looking as ugly as the very devil; but when youre all right and quite yourself, youre what I should call attractive. That is, to the people in the marrying line, you understand. You go to bed and have a good nice rest; and then get up and look at yourself in the glass; and you won't feel so cheap.

Eliza *again looks at him, speechless, and does not stir.*

The look is quite lost on him: he eats his apple with a dreamy expression of happiness, as it is quite a good one.

Higgins (*a genial afterthought occurring to him*). I daresay my mother could find some chap or other who would do very well.

Liza. We were above that at the corner of Tottenham Court Road.

Higgins (*waking up*). What do you mean?

Liza. I sold flowers. I didn't sell myself. Now youve made a lady of me I'm not fit to sell anything else. I wish youd left me where you found me.

Higgins (*slinging the core of the apple decisively into the grate*). Tosh, Eliza. Don't you insult human relations by dragging all this can't about buying and selling into it. You needn't marry the fellow if you don't like him.

Liza. What else am I to do?

Higgins. Oh, lots of things. What about your old idea of a florist's shop? Pickering could set you up in one: he has lots of money. (*Chuckling*) He'll have to pay for all those togs you have been wearing today; and that, with the hire of the jewellery, will make a big hole in two hundred pounds. Why, six months ago you would have thought it the millennium to have a flower shop of your own. Come! youll be all right. I must clear off to bed: I'm devilish sleepy. By the way, I came down for something: I forget what it was.

Liza. Your slippers.

Higgins. Oh yes, of course. You shied them at me. (*He picks them up, and is going out when she rises and speaks to him.*)

Liza. Before you go, sir—

Higgins (*dropping the slippers in his surprise at her calling him* Sir) Eh?

Liza. Do my clothes belong to me or to Colonel Pickering?

Higgins (*coming back into the room as if her question were the very climax of unreason*). What the devil use would they be to Pickering?

Liza. He might want them for the next girl you pick up to experiment on.

Higgins (*shocked and hurt*). Is that the way you feel towards us?

Liza. I don't want to hear anything more about that. All I want to know is whether anything belongs to me. My own clothes were burnt.

Higgins. But what does it matter? Why need you start bothering about that in the middle of the night?

Liza. I want to know what I may take away with me. I don't want to be accused of stealing.

Higgins (*now deeply wounded*). Stealing! You shouldn't have said that, Eliza. That shews a want of feeling.

Liza. I'm sorry. I'm only a common ignorant girl; and in my station I have to be careful. There can't be any feelings between the like of you and the like of me. Please will you tell me what belongs to me and what doesnt?

Higgins (*very sulky*). You may take the whole damned houseful if you like. Except the jewels. Theyre hired. Will that satisfy you? (*He turns on his heel and is about to go in extreme dudgeon.*)

Liza (*drinking in his emotion like nectar, and nagging him to provoke a further supply*). Stop, please. (*She takes off her jewels.*) Will you take these to your room and keep them safe? I don't want to run the risk of their being missing.

Higgins (*furious*). Hand them over. (*She puts them into his hands.*) If these belonged to me instead of to the jeweller, I'd ram them down your ungrateful throat. (*He perfunctorily thrusts them into his pockets, unconsciously decorating himself with the protruding ends of the chains.*)

Liza (*taking a ring off*). This ring isn't the jeweller's: it's the one you bought me in Brighton. I don't want it now. (*Higgins dashes the ring violently into the fireplace, and turns on her so threateningly that she crouches over the piano with her hands over her face, and exclaims.*) Don't you hit me.

Higgins. Hit you! You infamous creature, how dare you accuse me of such a thing? It is you who have hit me. You have wounded me to the heart.

Liza (*thrilling with hidden joy*). I'm glad. I've got a little of my own back, anyhow.

Higgins (*with dignity, in his finest professional style*). You have caused me to lose my temper: a thing that has hardly ever happened to me before. I prefer to say nothing more tonight. I am going to bed.

Liza (*pertly*). Youd better leave a note for Mrs. Pearce about the coffee; for she won't be told by me.

Higgins (*formally*). Damn Mrs. Pearce; and damn the coffee; and damn you; and (*wildly*) damn my own folly in having lavished my hard-earned knowledge and the treasure of my regard and intimacy on a heartless guttersnipe. (*He goes out with impressive decorum, and spoils it by slamming the door savagely.*)

Eliza goes down on her knees on the hearthrug to look for the ring. When she finds it she considers for a moment what to do with it. Finally she flings it down on the dessert stand and goes upstairs in a tearing rage.

The furniture of Eliza's room has been increased by a big wardrobe and a sumptuous dressing-table. She comes in and switches on the electric light. She goes to the wardrobe; opens it; and pulls out a walking dress, a hat, and a pair of shoes, which she throws on the bed. She takes off her evening dress and shoes; then takes a padded hanger from the wardrobe; adjusts it carefully in the evening dress; and hangs it in the wardrobe, which she shuts with a slam. She puts on her walking shoes, her walking dress, and hat. She takes her wrist watch from the dressing-table and fastens it on. She pulls on her gloves; takes her vanity bag; and looks into it to see that her purse is there before hanging it on her wrist. She makes for the door. Every movement expresses her furious resolution.

She takes a last look at herself in the glass.

She suddenly puts out her tongue at herself; then leaves the room, switching off the electric light at the door.

Meanwhile, in the street outside Freddy Eynsford Hill, *lovelorn, is gazing up at the second floor, in which one of the windows is still lighted.*

The light goes out.

Freddy. Goodnight, darling, darling, darling.

Eliza *comes out, giving the door a considerable bang behind her.*

Liza. Whatever are you doing here?

Freddy. Nothing. I spend most of my nights here. It's the only place where I'm happy. Don't laugh at me, Miss Doolittle.

Liza. Don't you call me Miss Doolittle, do you hear? Liza's good enough for me. (*She breaks down and grabs him by the shoulders.*) Freddy: you don't think I'm a heartless guttersnipe, do you?

Freddy. Oh no, no, darling: how can you imagine such a thing? You are the loveliest, dearest—

He loses all self-control and smothers her with kisses. She, hungry for comfort, responds. They stand there in one another's arms.

An elderly police constable arrives.

Constable (*scandalized*). Now then! Now then!! Now then!!!

They release one another hastily.

Freddy. Sorry, constable. Weve only just become engaged.

They run away.

The constable shakes his head, reflecting on his own courtship and on the vanity of human hopes. He moves off in the opposite direction with slow professional steps.

The flight of the lovers takes them to Cavendish Square. There they halt to consider their next move.

Liza (*out of breath*). He didn't half give me a fright, that copper. But you answered him proper.

Freddy. I hope I havn't taken you out of your way. Where were you going?

Liza. To the river.

Freddy. What for?

Liza. To make a hole in it.

Freddy (*horrified*). Eliza, darling. What do you mean? What's the matter?

Liza. Never mind. It doesn't matter now. Theres nobody in the world now but you and me, is there?

Freddy. Not a soul.

They indulge in another embrace, and are again surprised by a much younger constable.

Second Constable. Now then, you two! What's this? Where do you think you are? Move along here, double quick.

Freddy. As you say, sir, double quick.

They run away again, and are in Hanover Square before they stop for another conference.

Freddy. I had no idea the police were so devilishly prudish.

Liza. It's their business to hunt girls off the streets.

Freddy. We must go somewhere. We can't wander about the streets all night.

Liza. Can't we? I think it'd be lovely to wander about for ever.

Freddy. Oh, darling.

They embrace again, oblivious of the arrival of a crawling taxi. It stops.

Taximan. Can I drive you and the lady anywhere, sir?

They start asunder.

Liza. Oh, Freddy, a taxi. The very thing.

Freddy. But, damn it, I've no money.

Liza. I have plenty. The Colonel thinks you should never go out without ten pounds in your pocket. Listen. We'll drive about all night; and in the morning I'll call on old Mrs. Higgins and ask her what I ought to do. I'll tell you all about it in the cab. And the police won't touch us there.

Freddy. Righto! Ripping. (*To the* Taximan) Wimbledon Common. (*They drive off.*)

FIVE

Mrs. Higgins's drawing room. She is at her writing-table as before. The parlormaid comes in.

The Parlormaid (*at the door*). Mr. Henry, maam, is downstairs with Colonel Pickering.

Mrs. Higgins. Well, shew them up.

The Parlormaid. Theyre using the telephone, maam. Telephoning to the police, I think.

Mrs. Higgins. What!

The Parlormaid (*coming further in and lowering her voice*). Mr. Henry is in a state, maam. I thought I'd better tell you.

Mrs. Higgins. If you had told me that Mr. Henry was not in a state it would have been more surprising. Tell them to come up when theyve finished with the police. I suppose he's lost something.

The Parlormaid. Yes, maam. (*going*)

Mrs. Higgins. Go upstairs and tell Miss Doolittle that Mr. Henry and the Colonel are here. Ask her not to come down til I send for her.

The Parlormaid. Yes, maam.

Higgins bursts in. He is, as the parlormaid has said, in a state.

Higgins. Look here, mother: heres a confounded thing!

Mrs. Higgins. Yes, dear. Good morning. (*He checks his impatience and kisses her, whilst the parlormaid goes out.*) What is it?

Higgins. Eliza's bolted.

Mrs. Higgins (*calmly continuing her writing*). You must have frightened her.

Higgins. Frightened her! nonsense! She was left last night, as usual, to turn out the lights and all that; and instead of going to bed she changed her clothes and went right off: her bed wasn't slept in. She came in a cab for her things before seven this morning; and that fool Mrs. Pearce let her have them without telling me a word about it. What am I to do?

Mrs. Higgins. Do without, I'm afraid, Henry. The girl has a perfect right to leave if she chooses.

Higgins (*wandering distractedly across the room*). But I can't find anything. I don't know what appointments I've got. I'm—(Pickering *comes in.* Mrs. Higgins *puts down her pen and turns away from the writing-table.*)

Pickering (*shaking hands*). Good morning, Mrs. Higgins. Has Henry told you? (*He sits down on the ottoman.*)

Higgins. What does that ass of an inspector say? Have you offered a reward?

Mrs. Higgins (*rising in indignant amazement*). You don't mean to say you have set the police after Eliza?

Higgins. Of course. What are the police for? What else could we do? (*He sits in the Elizabethan chair.*)

Pickering. The inspector made a lot of difficulties. I really think he suspected us of some improper purpose.

Mrs. Higgins. Well, of course he did. What right have you to go to the police and give the girl's name as if she were a thief, or a lost umbrella, or something? Really! (*She sits down again, deeply vexed.*)

Higgins. But we want to find her.

Pickering. We can't let her go like this, you know, Mrs. Higgins. What were we to do?

Mrs. Higgins. You have no more sense, either of you, than two children. Why—

The parlormaid comes in and breaks off the conversation.

The Parlormaid. Mr. Henry: a gentleman wants to see you very particular. He's been sent on from Wimpole Street.

Higgins. Oh, bother! I can't see anyone now. Who is it?

The Parlormaid. A Mr. Doolittle, sir.

Pickering. Doolittle! Do you mean the dustman?

The Parlormaid. Dustman! Oh no, sir: a gentleman.

Higgins (*springing up excitedly*). By George, Pick, it's some relative of hers that she's gone to. Somebody we know nothing about. (*To the* Parlormaid) Send him up, quick.

The Parlormaid. Yes, sir. (*She goes.*)

Higgins (*eagerly, going to his mother*). Genteel relatives! now we shall hear something. (*He sits down in the Chippendale chair.*)

Mrs. Higgins. Do you know any of her people?

Pickering. Only her father: the fellow we told you about.

The Parlormaid (*announcing*). Mr. Doolittle. (*She withdraws.*)

Doolittle *enters. He is resplendently dressed as for a fashionable wedding, and might, in fact, be the bridegroom. A flower in his buttonhole, a dazzling silk hat, and patent leather shoes complete the effect. He is too concerned with the business he has come on to notice* Mrs. Higgins. *He walks straight to Higgins, and accosts him with vehement reproach.*

Doolittle (*indicating his own person*). See here! Do you see this? You done this.

Higgins. Done what, man?

Doolittle. This, I tell you. Look at it. Look at this hat. Look at this coat.

Pickering. Has Eliza been buying you clothes?

Doolittle. Eliza! not she. Why would she buy me clothes?

Mrs. Higgins. Good morning, Mr. Doolittle. Won't you sit down?

Doolittle (*taken aback as he becomes conscious that he has forgotten his hostess*). Asking your pardon, maam. (*He approaches her and shakes her proffered hand.*) Thank you. (*He sits down on the ottoman, on* Pickering's *right.*) I am that full of what has happened to me that I can't think of anything else.

Higgins. What the dickens has happened to you?

Doolittle. I shouldn't mind if it had only happened to me: anything might happen to anybody and nobody to blame but Providence, as you might say. But this is something that you done to me: yes, you, Enry Iggins.

Higgins. Have you found Eliza?

Doolittle. Have you lost her?

Higgins. Yes.

Doolittle. You have all the luck, you have. I ain't found her; but she'll find me quick enough now after what you done to me.

Mrs. Higgins. But what has my son done to you, Mr. Doolittle?

Doolittle. Done to me! Ruined me. Destroyed my happiness. Tied me up and delivered me into the hands of middle class morality.

Higgins (*rising intolerantly and standing over* Doolittle). Youre raving. Youre drunk. Youre mad. I gave you five pounds. After that I had two conversations with you, at half-a-crown an hour. I've never seen you since.

Doolittle. Oh! Drunk am I? Mad am I? Tell me this. Did you or did you not write a letter to an old blighter in America that was giving five millions to found Moral Reform Societies all over the world, and that wanted you to invent a universal language for him?

Higgins. What! Ezra D. Wannafeller! He's dead. (*He sits down again carelessly.*)

Doolittle. Yes: he's dead; and I'm done for. Now did you or did you not write a letter to him to say that the most original moralist at present in England, to the best of your knowledge, was Alfred Doolittle, a common dustman?

Higgins. Oh, after your first visit I remember making some silly joke of the kind.

Doolittle. Ah! You may well call it a silly joke. It put the lid on me right enough. Just give him the chance he wanted to shew that Americans is not like us: that they reckonize and respect merit in every class of life, however humble. Them words is in his blooming will, in which, Henry Higgins, thanks to your silly joking, he leaves me a share in his Pre-digested Cheese Trust worth three thousand a year on condition that I lecture for his Wannafeller Moral Reform World League as often as they ask me up to six times a year.

Higgins. The devil he does! Whew! (*Brightening suddenly*) What a lark!

Pickering. A safe thing for you, Doolittle. They won't ask you twice.

Doolittle. It ain't the lecturing I mind. I'll lecture them blue in the face, I will, and not turn a hair. It's making a gentleman of me that I object to. Who asked him to make a gentleman of me? I was happy. I was free. I touched pretty nigh everybody for money when I wanted it, same as I touched you, Enry Iggins. Now I am worrited; tied neck and heels; and everybody touches me for money. It's a fine thing for you, says my solicitor. Is it? says I. You mean it's a good thing for you, I says. When I was a poor man and had a solicitor once when they found a pram in the dust cart, he got me off, and got shut of me and got me shut of him as quick as he could. Same with the doctors: used to shove me out of the hospital before I could hardly stand on my legs, and nothing to pay. Now they finds out that I'm not a healthy man and can't live unless they looks after me twice a day. In the house I'm not let do a hand's turn for myself: somebody else must do it and touch me for it. A year ago I hadn't a relative in the world except two or three that wouldn't speak to me. Now I've fifty, and not a decent week's wages among the lot of them. I have to live for others and not for myself: thats middle class morality. You talk of losing Eliza. Don't you be anxious: I bet she's on my doorstep by this: she that could support herself easy by selling flowers if I wasn't respectable. And the next one to touch me will be you, Enry Iggins. I'll have to learn to speak middle class language from you, instead of speaking proper English. Thats where youll come in; and I daresay thats what you done it for.

Mrs. Higgins. But, my dear Mr. Doolittle, you need not suffer all this if you are really in earnest. Nobody can force you to accept this bequest. You can repudiate it. Isn't that so, Colonel Pickering?

Pickering. I believe so.

Doolittle (*softening his manner in deference to her sex*). Thats the tragedy of it, maam. It's easy to say chuck it; but I havn't the nerve. Which of us has? We're all intimidated. Intimidated, maam: thats what we are. What is there for me if I chuck it but the workhouse in my old age? I have to dye my hair already to keep my job as a dustman. If I was one of the deserving poor, and had put by a bit, I could chuck it; but then why should I, acause the deserving poor might as well be millionaires for all the happiness they ever has. They don't know what happiness is. But I, as one of the undeserving poor, have nothing between me and the pauper's uniform but this here blasted three thousand a year that shoves me into the middle class. (Excuse the expression, maam; youd use it yourself if you had my provocation.) Theyve got you every way you turn: it's a choice between the Skilly of the workhouse and the Char Bydis of the middle class; and I havn't the nerve for the workhouse. Intimidated: thats what I am. Broke. Bought up. Happier men than me will call for my dust, and touch me for their tip; and I'll look on helpless, and envy them. And thats what your son has brought me to. (*He is overcome by emotion.*)

Mrs. Higgins. Well, I'm very glad youre not going to do anything foolish, Mr. Doolittle. For this solves the problem of Eliza's future. You can provide for her now.

Doolittle (*with melancholy resignation*). Yes, maam: I'm expected to provide for everyone now, out of three thousand a year.

Higgins (*jumping up*) Nonsense! he can't provide for her. He shan't provide for her. She doesn't belong to him. I paid him five pounds for her. Doolittle: either youre an honest man or a rogue.

Doolittle (*tolerantly*). A little of both, Henry, like the rest of us: a little of both.

Higgins. Well, you took that money for the girl; and you have no right to take her as well.

Mrs. Higgins. Henry: don't be absurd. If you want to know where Eliza is, she is upstairs.

Higgins (*amazed*). Upstairs!!! Then I shall jolly soon fetch her downstairs. (*He makes resolutely for the door.*)

Mrs. Higgins (*rising and following him*). Be quiet, Henry. Sit down.

Higgins. I—

Mrs. Higgins. Sit down, dear; and listen to me.

Higgins. Oh very well, very well, very well. (*He throws himself ungraciously on the ottoman, with his face* *towards the windows.*) But I think you might have told us this half an hour ago.

Mrs. Higgins. Eliza came to me this morning. She told me of the brutal way you two treated her.

Higgins (*bouncing up again*). What!

Pickering (*rising also*). My dear Mrs. Higgins, she's been telling you stories. We didn't treat her brutally. We hardly said a word to her; and we parted on particularly good terms. (*Turning on* Higgins) Higgins: did you bully her after I went to bed?

Higgins. Just the other way about. She threw my slippers in my face. She behaved in the most outrageous way. I never gave her the slightest provocation. The slippers came bang into my face the moment I entered the room—before I had uttered a word. And used perfectly awful language.

Pickering (*astonished*). But why? What did we do to her?

Mrs. Higgins. I think I know pretty well what you did. The girl is naturally rather affectionate, I think. Isn't she, Mr. Doolittle?

Doolittle. Very tender-hearted, maam. Takes after me.

Mrs. Higgins. Just so. She had become attached to you both. She worked very hard for you, Henry. I don't think you quite realize what anything in the nature of brain work means to a girl of her class. Well, it seems that when the great day of trial came, and she did this wonderful thing for you without making a single mistake, you two sat there and never said a word to her, but talked together of how glad you were that it was all over and how you had been bored with the whole thing. And then you were surprised because she threw your slippers at you! I should have thrown the fire-irons at you.

Higgins. We said nothing except that we were tired and wanted to go to bed. Did we, Pick?

Pickering (*shrugging his shoulders*). That was all.

Mrs. Higgins (*ironically*). Quite sure?

Pickering. Absolutely. Really, that was all.

Mrs. Higgins. You didn't thank her, or pet her, or admire her, or tell her how splendid she'd been.

Higgins (*impatiently*). But she knew all about that. We didn't make speeches to her, if thats what you mean.

Pickering (*conscience stricken*). Perhaps we were a little inconsiderate. Is she very angry?

Mrs. Higgins (*returning to her place at the writing-table*). Well, I'm afraid she won't go back to Wimpole Street, especially now that Mr. Doolittle is able to keep up the position you have thrust on her; but she says she is quite willing to meet you on friendly terms and to let bygones be bygones.

Higgins (*furious*). Is she, by George? Ho!

Mrs. Higgins. If you promise to behave yourself, Henry, I'll ask her to come down. If not, go home; for you have taken up quite enough of my time.

Higgins. Oh, all right. Very well. Pick: you behave yourself. Let us put on our best Sunday manners for this creature that we picked out of the mud. (*He flings himself sulkily into the Elizabethan chair.*)

Doolittle (*remonstrating*). Now, now, Enry Iggins! Have some consideration for my feelings as a middle class man.

Mrs. Higgins. Remember your promise, Henry. (*She presses the bell-button on the writing-table.*) Mr. Doolittle: will you be so good as to step out on the balcony for a moment. I don't want Eliza to have the shock of your news until she has made it up with these two gentlemen. Would you mind?

Doolittle. As you wish, lady. Anything to help Henry to keep her off my hands. (*He disappears through the window.*)

The parlormaid answers the bell. Pickering *sits down in* Doolittle's *place.*

Mrs. Higgins. Ask Miss Doolittle to come down, please.

The Parlormaid. Yes, maam. (*She goes out.*)

Mrs. Higgins. Now, Henry: be good.

Higgins. I am behaving myself perfectly.

Pickering. He is doing his best, Mrs. Higgins.

A pause. Higgins *throws back his head; stretches out his legs; and begins to whistle.*

Mrs. Higgins. Henry, dearest, you don't look at all nice in that attitude.

Higgins (*pulling himself together*). I was not trying to look nice, mother.

Mrs. Higgins. It doesn't matter, dear. I only wanted to make you speak.

Higgins. Why?

Mrs. Higgins. Because you can't speak and whistle at the same time.

Higgins *groans. Another very trying pause.*

Higgins (*springing up, out of patience*). Where the devil is that girl? Are we to wait here all day?

Eliza enters, sunny, self-possessed, and giving a staggeringly convincing exhibition of ease of manner. She carries a little work-basket, and is very much at home. Pickering *is too much taken aback to rise.*

Liza. How do you do, Professor Higgins? Are you quite well?

Higgins (*choking*). Am I—(*He can say no more.*)

Liza. But of course you are: you are never ill. So glad to see you again, Colonel Pickering. (*He rises hastily; and they shake hands.*) Quite chilly this morning, isn't it? (*She sits down on his left. He sits beside her.*)

Higgins. Don't you dare try this game on me. I taught it to you; and it doesn't take me in. Get up and come home; and don't be a fool.

Eliza takes a piece of needlework from her basket, and begins to stitch at it, without taking the least notice of this outburst.

Mrs. Higgins. Very nicely put, indeed, Henry. No woman could resist such an invitation.

Higgins. You let her alone, mother. Let her speak for herself. You will jolly soon see whether she has an idea that I havn't put into her head or a word that I havn't put into her mouth. I tell you I have created this thing out of the squashed cabbage leaves of Covent Garden; and now she pretends to play the fine lady with me.

Mrs. Higgins (*placidly*). Yes, dear; but youll sit down, won't you?

Higgins sits down again, savagely.

Liza (to Pickering, *taking no apparent notice of* Higgins, *and working away deftly*). Will you drop me altogether now that the experiment is over, Colonel Pickering?

Pickering. Oh dont. You mustn't think of it as an experiment. It shocks me, somehow.

Liza. Oh, I'm only a squashed cabbage leaf—

Pickering (*impulsively*). No.

Liza (*continuing quietly*). —but I owe so much to you that I should be very unhappy if you forgot me.

Pickering. It's very kind of you to say so, Miss Doolittle.

Liza. It's not because you paid for my dresses. I know you are generous to everybody with money. But it was from you that I learn't really nice manners; and that is what makes one a lady, isn't it? You see it was so very difficult for me with the example of Professor Higgins always before me. I was brought up to be just like him, unable to control myself, and using bad language on the slightest provocation. And I should never have known that ladies and gentlemen didn't behave like that if you hadn't been there.

Higgins. Well!!

Pickering. Oh, thats only his way, you know. He doesn't mean it.

Liza. Oh, I didn't mean it either, when I was a flower girl. It was only my way. But you see I did it; and thats what makes the difference after all.

Pickering. No doubt. Still, he taught you to speak; and I couldn't have done that, you know.

Liza (*trivially*). Of course: that is his profession.

Higgins. Damnation!

Liza (*continuing*). It was just like learning to dance in the fashionable way: there was nothing more than that in it. But do you know what began my real education?

Pickering. What?

Liza (*stopping her work for a moment*). Your calling me Miss Doolittle that day when I first came to Wimpole Street. That was the beginning of self-respect for me. (*She resumes her stitching.*) And there were a hundred little things you never noticed, because they came naturally to you. Things about standing up and taking off your hat and opening doors—

Pickering. Oh, that was nothing.

Liza. Yes: things that shewed you thought and felt about me as if I were something better than a scullery-maid; though of course I know you would have been just the same to a scullery-maid if she had been let into the drawing room. You never took off your boots in the dining room when I was there.

Pickering. You mustn't mind that. Higgins takes off his boots all over the place.

Liza. I know. I am not blaming him. It is his way, isn't it? But it made such a difference to me that you didn't do it. You see, really and truly, apart from the things anyone can pick up (the dressing and the proper way of speaking, and so on), the difference between a lady and a flower girl is not how she behaves, but how she's treated. I shall always be a flower girl to Professor Higgins, because he always treats me as a flower girl, and always will; but I know I can be a lady to you, because you always treat me as a lady, and always will.

Mrs. Higgins. Please don't grind your teeth, Henry.

Pickering. Well, this is really very nice of you, Miss Doolittle.

Liza. I should like you to call me Eliza, now, if you would.

Pickering. Thank you. Eliza, of course.

Liza. And I should like Professor Higgins to call me Miss Doolittle.

Higgins. I'll see you damned first.

Mrs. Higgins. Henry! Henry!

Pickering (*laughing*). Why don't you slang back at him? Don't stand it. It would do him a lot of good.

Liza. I cant. I could have done it once but now I can't go back to it. You told me, you know, that when a child is brought to a foreign country, it picks up the language in a few weeks, and forgets its own. Well, I am a child in your country. I have forgotten my own language, and can speak nothing but yours. Thats the real break-off with the corner of Tottenham Court Road. Leaving Wimpole Street finishes it.

Pickering (*much alarmed*). Oh! but youre coming back to Wimpole Street, arn't you? Youll forgive Higgins?

Higgins (*rising*). Forgive! Will she, by George! Let her go. Let her find out how she can get on without us. She will relapse into the gutter in three weeks without me at her elbow.

Doolittle *appears at the centre window. With a look of dignified reproach at* Higgins, *he comes slowly and silently to his daughter, who, with her back to the window, is unconscious of his approach.*

Pickering. He's incorrigible, Eliza. You won't relapse, will you?

Liza. No: not now. Never again. I have learnt my lesson. I don't believe I could utter one of the old sounds if I tried. (Doolittle *touches her on her left shoulder. She drops her work, losing her self-possession utterly at the spectacle of her father's splendor.*) A-a-a-a-a-ah-ow-ooh!

Higgins (*with a crow of triumph*). Aha! Just so. A-a-a-a-ahowooh! A-a-a-a-ahowooh! A-a-a-a-ahowooh! Victory! Victory! (*He throws himself on the divan, folding his arms, and spraddling arrogantly.*)

Doolittle. Can you blame the girl? Don't look at me like that, Eliza. It ain't my fault. I've come into some money.

Liza. You must have touched a millionaire this time, dad.

Doolittle. I have. But I'm dressed something special today. I'm going to St George's, Hanover Square. Your stepmother is going to marry me.

Liza (*angrily*). Youre going to let yourself down to marry that low common woman!

Pickering (*quietly*). He ought to, Eliza. (*To* Doolittle) Why has she changed her mind?

Doolittle (*sadly*). Intimidated, Governor. Intimidated. Middle class morality claims its victim. Won't you put on your hat, Liza, and come and see me turned off?

Liza. If the Colonel says I must, I—I'll (*almost sobbing*) I'll demean myself. And get insulted for my pains, like enough.

Doolittle. Don't be afraid: she never comes to words with anyone now, poor woman! respectability has broke all the spirit out of her.

Pickering (*squeezing* Eliza's *elbow gently*). Be kind to them, Eliza. Make the best of it.

Liza (*forcing a little smile for him through her vexation*). Oh well, just to shew theres no ill feeling. I'll be back in a moment. (*She goes out.*)

Doolittle (*sitting down beside* Pickering). I feel uncommon nervous about the ceremony, Colonel. I wish youd come and see me through it.

Pickering. But youve been through it before, man. You were married to Eliza's mother.

Doolittle. Who told you that, Colonel?

Pickering. Well, nobody told me. But I concluded—naturally—

Doolittle. No: that ain't the natural way, Colonel: it's only the middle class way. My way was always the undeserving way. But don't say nothing to Eliza. She don't know: I always had a delicacy about telling her.

Pickering. Quite right. We'll leave it so, if you don't mind.

Doolittle. And youll come to the church, Colonel, and put me through straight?

Pickering. With pleasure. As far as a bachelor can.

Mrs. Higgins. May I come, Mr. Doolittle? I should be very sorry to miss your wedding.

Doolittle. I should indeed be honored by your condescension, maam; and my poor old woman would take it as a tremenjous compliment. She's been very low, thinking of the happy days that are no more.

Mrs. Higgins (*rising*). I'll order the carriage and get ready. (*The men rise, except* Higgins.) I shan't be more than fifteen minutes. (*As she goes to the door* Eliza *comes in, hatted and buttoning her gloves.*) I'm going to the church to see your father married, Eliza. You had better come in the brougham with me. Colonel Pickering can go on with the bridegroom.

Mrs. Higgins *goes out.* Eliza *comes to the middle of the room between the centre window and the ottoman.* Pickering *joins her.*

Doolittle. Bridegroom! What a word! It makes a man realize his position, somehow. (*He takes up his hat and goes towards the door.*)

Pickering. Before I go, Eliza, do forgive Higgins and come back to us.

Liza. I don't think dad would allow me. Would you, dad?

Doolittle (*sad but magnanimous*). They played you off very cunning, Eliza, them two sportsmen. If it had been only one of them, you could have nailed him. But you see, there was two; and one of them chaperoned the other, as you might say. (*To* Pickering) It was artful of you, Colonel; but I bear no malice: I should have done the same myself. I been the victim of one woman after another all my life, and I don't grudge you two getting the better of Liza. I shan't interfere. It's time for us to go, Colonel. So long, Henry. See you in St George's, Eliza. (*He goes out.*)

Pickering (*coaxing*). Do stay with us, Eliza. (*He follows Doolittle.*)

Eliza goes out on the balcony to avoid being alone with Higgins. He rises and joins her there. She immediately comes back into the room and makes for the door; but he goes along the balcony quickly and gets his back to the door before she reaches it.

Higgins. Well, Eliza, youve had a bit of your own back, as you call it. Have you had enough? and are you going to be reasonable? Or do you want any more?

Liza. You want me back only to pick up your slippers and put up with your tempers and fetch and carry for you.

Higgins. I havn't said I wanted you back at all.

Liza. Oh, indeed. Then what are we talking about?

Higgins. About you, not about me. If you come back I shall treat you just as I have always treated you. I can't change my nature; and I don't intend to change my manners. My manners are exactly the same as Colonel Pickering's.

Liza. Thats not true. He treats a flower girl as if she was a duchess.

Higgins. And I treat a duchess as if she was a flower girl.

Liza. I see. (*She turns away composedly, and sits on the ottoman, facing the window.*) The same to everybody.

Higgins. Just so.

Liza. Like father.

Higgins (*grinning, a little taken down*). Without accepting the comparison at all points, Eliza, it's quite true that your father is not a snob, and that he will be quite at home in any station of life to which his eccentric destiny may call him. (*Seriously*) The great secret, Eliza, is not having bad manners or good manners or any other particular sort of manners, but having the same manner for all human souls: in short, behaving as if you were in Heaven, where there are no third-class carriages, and one soul is as good as another.

Liza. Amen. You are a born preacher.

Higgins (*irritated*). The question is not whether I treat you rudely, but whether you ever heard me treat anyone else better.

Liza (*with sudden sincerity*). I don't care how you treat me. I don't mind your swearing at me. I shouldn't mind a black eye: I've had one before this. But (*standing up and facing him*) I won't be passed over.

Higgins. Then get out of my way; for I won't stop for you. You talk about me as if I were a motor bus.

Liza. So you are a motor bus: all bounce and go, and no consideration for anyone. But I can do without you: don't think I cant.

Higgins. I know you can. I told you you could.

Liza (*wounded, getting away from him to the other side of the ottoman with her face to the hearth*). I know you did, you brute. You wanted to get rid of me.

Higgins. Liar.

Liza. Thank you. (*She sits down with dignity.*)

Higgins. You never asked yourself, I suppose, whether I could do without you.

Liza (*earnestly*). Don't you try to get round me. Youll have to do without me.

Higgins (*arrogant*). I can do without anybody. I have my own soul: my own spark of divine fire. But (*with sudden humility*) I shall miss you, Eliza. (*He sits down near her on the ottoman.*) I have learnt something from your idiotic notions: I confess that humbly and gratefully. And I have grown accustomed to your voice and appearance. I like them, rather.

Liza. Well, you have both of them on your gramophone and in your book of photographs. When you feel lonely without me, you can turn the machine on. It's got no feelings to hurt.

Higgins. I can't turn your soul on. Leave me those feelings; and you can take away the voice and the face. They are not you.

Liza. Oh, you are a devil. You can twist the heart in a girl as easy as some could twist her arms to hurt her. Mrs. Pearce warned me. Time and again she has wanted to leave you; and you always got round her at the last minute. And you don't care a bit for her. And you don't care a bit for me.

Higgins. I care for life, for humanity; and you are a part of it that has come my way and been built into my house. What more can you or anyone ask?

Liza. I won't care for anybody that doesn't care for me.

Higgins. Commercial principles, Eliza. Like (*reproducing her Covent Garden pronunciation with professional exactness*) s'yollin voylets (*selling violets*), isn't it?

Liza. Don't sneer at me. It's mean to sneer at me.

Higgins. I have never sneered in my life. Sneering

doesn't become either the human face or the human soul. I am expressing my righteous contempt for Commercialism. I don't and wont trade in affection. You call me a brute because you couldn't buy a claim on me by fetching my slippers and finding my spectacles. You were a fool: I think a woman fetching a man's slippers is a disgusting sight: did I ever fetch your slippers? I think a good deal more of you for throwing them in my face. No use slaving for me and then saying you want to be cared for: who cares for a slave? If you come back, come back for the sake of good fellowship; for youll get nothing else. Youve had a thousand times as much out of me as I have out of you; and if you dare to set up your little dog's tricks of fetching and carrying slippers against my creation of a Duchess Eliza, I'll slam the door in your silly face.

Liza. What did you do it for if you didn't care for me?

Higgins (*heartily*). Why, because it was my job.

Liza. You never thought of the trouble it would make for me.

Higgins. Would the world ever have been made if its maker had been afraid of making trouble? Making life means making trouble. Theres only one way of escaping trouble; and thats killing things. Cowards, you notice, are always shrieking to have troublesome people killed.

Liza. I'm no preacher: I don't notice things like that. I notice that you don't notice me.

Higgins (*jumping up and walking about intolerantly*). Eliza: youre an idiot. I waste the treasures of my Miltonic mind by spreading them before you. Once for all, understand that I go my way and do my work without caring twopence what happens to either of us. I am not intimidated, like your father and your stepmother. So you can come back or go to the devil: which you please.

Liza. What am I to come back for?

Higgins (*bouncing up on his knees on the ottoman and leaning over it to her*). For the fun of it. Thats why I took you on.

Liza (*with averted face*). And you may throw me out tomorrow if I don't do everything you want me to?

Higgins. Yes; and you may walk out tomorrow if I don't do everything you want me to.

Liza. And live with my stepmother?

Higgins. Yes, or sell flowers.

Liza. Oh! If I only could go back to my flower basket! I should be independent of both you and father and all the world! Why did you take my independence from me? Why did I give it up? I'm a slave now, for all my fine clothes.

Higgins. Not a bit. I'll adopt you as my daughter and settle money on you if you like. Or would you rather marry Pickering?

Liza (*looking fiercely round at him*). I wouldn't marry you if you asked me; and youre nearer my age than what he is.

Higgins (*gently*). Than he is: not 'than what he is'.

Liza (*losing her temper and rising*). I'll talk as I like. Youre not my teacher now.

Higgins (*reflectively*). I don't suppose Pickering would, though. He's as confirmed an old bachelor as I am.

Liza. Thats not what I want; and don't you think it. I've always had chaps enough wanting me that way. Freddy Hill writes to me twice and three times a day, sheets and sheets.

Higgins (*disagreeably surprised*). Damn his impudence! (*He recoils and finds himself sitting on his heels.*)

Liza. He has a right to if he likes, poor lad. And he does love me.

Higgins (*getting off the ottoman*). You have no right to encourage him.

Liza. Every girl has a right to be loved.

Higgins. What! By fools like that?

Liza. Freddy's not a fool. And if he's weak and poor and wants me, may be he'd make me happier than my betters that bully me and don't want me.

Higgins. Can he make anything of you? Thats the point.

Liza. Perhaps I could make something of him. But I never thought of us making anything of one another; and you never think of anything else. I only want to be natural.

Higgins. In short, you want me to be as infatuated about you as Freddy? Is that it?

Liza. No I dont. Thats not the sort of feeling I want from you. And don't you be too sure of yourself or of me. I could have been a bad girl if I'd liked. I've seen more of some things than you, for all your learning. Girls like me can drag gentlemen down to make love to them easy enough. And they wish each other dead the next minute.

Higgins. Of course they do. Then what in thunder are we quarrelling about?

Liza (*much troubled*). I want a little kindness. I know I'm a common ignorant girl, and you a book-learned gentleman; but I'm not dirt under your feet. What I done (*correcting herself*) what I did was not for the dresses and the taxis: I did it because we were pleasant together and I come—came—to care for you; not to want you to make love to me, and not forgetting the difference between us, but more friendly like.

Higgins. Well, of course. Thats just how I feel. And how Pickering feels. Eliza: youre a fool.

Liza. Thats not a proper answer to give me. (*She sinks on the chair at the writing-table in tears.*)

Higgins. It's all youll get until you stop being a common idiot. If youre going to be a lady, youll have to give up feeling neglected if the men you know don't spend half their time snivelling over you and the other half giving you black eyes. If you can't stand the coldness of my sort of life, and the strain of it, go back to the gutter. Work til youre more a brute than a human being; and then cuddle and squabble and drink til you fall asleep. Oh, it's a fine life, the life of the gutter. It's real: it's warm: it's violent: you can feel it through the thickest skin: you can taste it and smell it without any training or any work. Not like Science and Literature and Classical Music and Philosophy and Art. You find me cold, unfeeling, selfish, don't you? Very well: be off with you to the sort of people you like. Marry some sentimental hog or other with lots of money, and a thick pair of lips to kiss you with and a thick pair of boots to kick you with. If you can't appreciate what youve got, youd better get what you can appreciate.

Liza (*desperate*). Oh, you are a cruel tyrant. I can't talk to you: you turn everything against me: I'm always in the wrong. But you know very well all the time that youre nothing but a bully. You know I can't go back to the gutter, as you call it, and that I have no real friends in the world but you and the Colonel. You know well I couldn't bear to live with a low common man after you two; and it's wicked and cruel of you to insult me by pretending I could. You think I must go back to Wimpole Street because I have nowhere else to go but father's. But don't you be too sure that you have me under your feet to be trampled on and talked down. I'll marry Freddy, I will, as soon as I'm able to support him.

Higgins (*thunderstruck*). Freddy!!! that young fool! That poor devil who couldn't get a job as an errand boy even if he had the guts to try for it! Woman: do you not understand that I have made you a consort for a king?

Liza. Freddy loves me: that makes him king enough for me. I don't want him to work: he wasn't brought up to it as I was. I'll go and be a teacher.

Higgins. Whatll you teach, in heaven's name?

Liza. What you taught me. I'll teach phonetics.

Higgins. Ha! ha! ha!

Liza. I'll offer myself as an assistant to that hairyfaced Hungarian.

Higgins (*rising in a fury*). What! That impostor! that humbug! that toadying ignoramus! Teach him my methods! my discoveries! You take one step in his direction and I'll wring your neck. (*He lays hands on her.*) Do you hear?

Liza (*defiantly non-resistant*). Wring away. What do I

care? I knew youd strike me some day. (*He lets her go, stamping with rage at having forgotten himself, and recoils so hastily that he stumbles back into his seat on the ottoman.*) Aha! Now I know how to deal with you. What a fool I was not to think of it before! You can't take away the knowledge you gave me. You said I had a finer ear than you. And I can be civil and kind to people, which is more than you can. Aha! (*Purposely dropping her aitches to annoy him*) Thats done you, Enry Iggins, it az. Now I don't care that (*snapping her fingers*) for your bullying and your big talk. I'll advertize it in the papers that your duchess is only a flower girl that you taught, and that she'll teach anybody to be a duchess just the same in six months for a thousand guineas. Oh, when I think of myself crawling under your feet and being trampled on and called names, when all the time I had only to lift up my finger to be as good as you, I could just kick myself.

Higgins (*wondering at her*). You damned impudent slut, you! But it's better than snivelling; better than fetching slippers and finding spectacles, isn't it? (*Rising*) By George, Eliza, I said I'd make a woman of you; and I have. I like you like this.

Liza. Yes: you can turn round and make up to me now that I'm not afraid of you, and can do without you.

Higgins. Of course I do, you little fool. Five minutes ago you were like a millstone round my neck. Now youre a tower of strength: a consort battleship. You and I and Pickering will be three old bachelors instead of only two men and a silly girl.

Mrs. Higgins *returns, dressed for the wedding.* Eliza *instantly becomes cool and elegant.*

Mrs. Higgins. The carriage is waiting, Eliza. Are you ready?

Liza. Quite. Is the Professor coming?

Mrs. Higgins. Certainly not. He can't behave himself in church. He makes remarks out loud all the time on the clergyman's pronunciation.

Liza. Then I shall not see you again, Professor. Goodbye. (*She goes to the door.*)

Mrs. Higgins (*coming to* Higgins). Goodbye, dear.

Higgins. Goodbye, mother. (*He is about to kiss her, when he recollects something.*) Oh, by the way, Eliza, order a ham and a Stilton cheese, will you? And buy me a pair of reindeer gloves, number eights, and a tie to match that new suit of mine. You can choose the color. (*His cheerful, careless, vigorous voice shews that he is incorrigible.*)

Liza (*disdainfully*). Number eights are too small for you if you want them lined with lamb's wool. You have three new ties that you have forgotten in the drawer of your washstand. Colonel Pickering prefers double Gloucester to Stilton; and you don't notice the difference. I telephoned Mrs. Pearce this morning not to forget the ham. What you are to do without me I cannot imagine. (*She sweeps out.*)

Mrs. Higgins. I'm afraid youve spoilt that girl, Henry. I should be uneasy about you and her if she were less fond of Colonel Pickering.

Higgins. Pickering! Nonsense: she's going to marry Freddy. Ha ha! Freddy! Freddy!! Ha ha ha ha ha!!!!!

(*He roars with laughter as the play ends.*)

The rest of the story need not be shewn in action, and indeed, would hardly need telling if our imaginations were not so enfeebled by their lazy dependence on the ready-mades and reach-me-downs of the ragshop in which Romance keeps its stock of 'happy endings' to misfit all stories. Now, the history of Eliza Doolittle, though called a romance because the transfiguration it records seems exceedingly improbable, is common enough. Such transfigurations have been achieved by hundreds of resolutely ambitious young women since Nell Gwynne set them the example by playing queens and fascinating kings in the theatre in which she began by selling oranges. Nevertheless, people in all directions have assumed, for no other reason than that she became the heroine of a romance, that she must have married the hero of it. This is unbearable, not only because her little drama, if acted on such a thoughtless assumption, must be spoiled, but because the true sequel is patent to anyone with a sense of human nature in general, and of feminine instinct in particular.

Eliza, in telling Higgins she would not marry him if he asked, was not coquetting: she was announcing a well-considered decision. When a bachelor interests, and dominates, and teaches, and becomes important to a spinster, as Higgins with Eliza, she always, if she has character enough to be capable of it, considers very seriously indeed whether she will play for becoming that bachelor's wife, especially if he is so little interested in marriage that a determined and devoted woman might capture him if she set herself resolutely to do it. Her decision will depend a good deal on whether she is really free to choose; and that, again, will depend on her age and income. If she is at the end of her youth, and has no security for her livelihood, she will marry him because she must marry anybody who will provide for her. But at Eliza's age a good-looking girl does not feel that pressure: she feels free to pick and choose. She is therefore guided by her instinct in the matter. Eliza's instinct tells her not to marry Higgins. It does not tell her to give him up. It is not in the slightest doubt as to his remaining one of the strongest personal interests in her life. It would be very sorely strained if there was another woman likely to supplant her with him. But as she feels sure of him on that last point, she has no doubt at all as to her course, and would not have any, even if the difference of twenty years in age, which seems so great to youth, did not exist between them.

As our own instincts are not appealed to by her conclusion, let us see whether we cannot discover some reason in it. When Higgins excused his indifference to young women on the ground that they had an irresistible rival in his mother, he gave the clue to his inveterate old-bachelordom. The case is uncommon only to the extent that remarkable mothers are uncommon. If an imaginative boy has a sufficiently rich mother who has intelligence, personal grace, dignity of character without harshness, and a cultivated sense of the best art of her time to enable her to make her house beautiful, she sets a standard for him against which very few women can struggle, besides effecting for him a disengagement of his affections, his sense of beauty, and his idealism from his specifically sexual impulses. This makes him a standing puzzle to the huge number of uncultivated people who have been brought up in tasteless homes by commonplace or disagreeable parents, and to whom, consequently, literature, painting, sculpture, music, and affectionate personal relations come as modes of sex if they come at all. The word passion means nothing else to them; and that Higgins could have a passion for phonetics and idealize his mother instead of Eliza, would seem to them absurd and unnatural. Nevertheless, when we look round and see that hardly anyone is too ugly or disagreeable to find a wife or a husband if he or she wants one, whilst many old maids and bachelors are above the average in quality and culture, we cannot help suspecting that the disentanglement of sex from the associations with which it is commonly confused, a disentanglement which persons of genius achieve by sheer intellectual analysis, is sometimes produced or aided by parental fascination.

Now, though Eliza was incapable of thus explaining to herself Higgins's formidable powers of resistance to the charm that prostrated Freddy at the first glance, she was instinctively aware that she could never obtain a complete grip of him, or come between him and his mother (the first necessity of the married woman). To put it shortly, she knew that for some mysterious reason he had not the makings of a married man in him, according to her conception of a husband as one to whom she would be his nearest and fondest and warmest interest. Even had there been no mother-rival, she would still have refused to accept an interest in herself that was secondary to philosophic interests. Had Mrs. Higgins died, there would still have been Milton and the Universal Alphabet. Landor's remark that to those who have the greatest power of loving, love is a secondary affair, would not have recommended Landor to Eliza. Put that along with her resentment of Higgins's domineering superiority, and her mistrust of his coaxing cleverness in getting round her and evading her wrath when he had gone too far with his impetuous bullying, and you will see that Eliza's instinct had good grounds for warning her not to marry her Pygmalion.

And now, whom did Eliza marry? For if Higgins was a predestinate old bachelor, she was most certainly not a predestinate old maid. Well, that can be told very shortly to those who have not guessed it from the indications she has herself given them.

Almost immediately after Eliza is stung into

proclaiming her considered determination not to marry Higgins, she mentions the fact that young Mr. Frederick Eynsford Hill is pouring out his love for her daily through the post. Now Freddy is young, practically twenty years younger than Higgins: he is a gentleman (or, as Eliza would qualify him, a toff), and speaks like one. He is nicely dressed, is treated by the Colonel as an equal, loves her unaffectedly, and is not her master, nor ever likely to dominate her in spite of his advantage of social standing. Eliza has no use for the foolish romantic tradition that all women love to be mastered, if not actually bullied and beaten. "When you go to women" says Nietzsche "take your whip with you." Sensible despots have never confined that precaution to women: they have taken their whips with them when they have dealt with men, and been slavishly idealized by the men over whom they have flourished the whip much more than by women. No doubt there are slavish women as well as slavish men; and women, like men, admire those that are stronger than themselves. But to admire a strong person and to live under that strong person's thumb are two different things. The weak may not be admired and hero-worshipped; but they are by no means disliked or shunned; and they never seem to have the least difficulty in marrying people who are too good for them. They may fail in emergencies; but life is not one long emergency: it is mostly a string of situations for which no exceptional strength is needed, and with which even rather weak people can cope if they have a stronger partner to help them out. Accordingly, it is a truth everywhere in evidence that strong people, masculine or feminine, not only do not marry stronger people, but do not shew any preference for them in selecting their friends. When a lion meets another with a louder roar "the first lion thinks the last a bore." The man or woman who feels strong enough for two, seeks for every other quality in a partner than strength.

The converse is also true. Weak people want to marry strong people who do not frighten them too much; and this often leads them to make the mistake we describe metaphorically as 'biting off more than they can chew'. They want too much for too little; and when the bargain is unreasonable beyond all bearing, the union becomes impossible: it ends in the weaker party being either discarded or borne as a cross, which is worse. People who are not only weak, but silly or obtuse as well, are often in these difficulties.

This being the state of human affairs, what is Eliza fairly sure to do when she is placed between Freddy and Higgins? Will she look forward to a lifetime of fetching Higgins's slippers or to a lifetime of Freddy fetching hers? There can be no doubt about the answer. Unless Freddy is biologically repulsive to her, and Higgins biologically attractive to a degree that overwhelms all her other instincts, she will, if she marries either of them, marry Freddy.

And that is just what Eliza did.

Complications ensued; but they were economic, not romantic. Freddy had no money and no occupation. His mother's jointure, a last relic of the opulence of Largelady Park, had enabled her to struggle along in Earlscourt with an air of gentility, but not to procure any serious secondary education for her children, much less give the boy a profession. A clerkship at thirty shillings a week was beneath Freddy's dignity, and extremely distasteful to him besides. His prospects consisted of a hope that if he kept up appearances somebody would do something for him. The something appeared vaguely to his imagination as a private secretaryship or a sinecure of some sort. To his mother it perhaps appeared as a marriage to some lady of means who could not resist her boy's niceness. Fancy her feelings when he married a flower girl who had become disclassed under extra-ordinary circumstances which were now notorious!

It is true that Eliza's situation did not seem wholly ineligible. Her father, though formerly a dustman, and now fantastically disclassed, had become extremely popular in the smartest society by a social talent which triumphed over every prejudice and every disadvantage. Rejected by the middle class, which he loathed, he had shot up at once into the highest circles by his wit, his dustmanship (which he carried like a banner), and his Nietzschean transcendence of good and evil. At intimate ducal dinners he sat on the right-hand of the Duchess; and in country houses he smoked in the pantry and was made much of by the butler when he was not feeding in the dining room and being consulted by cabinet ministers. But he found it almost as hard to do all this on four thousand a year as Mrs. Eynsford Hill to live in Earlscourt on an income so pitiably smaller that I have not the heart to disclose its exact figure. He absolutely refused to add the last straw to his burden by contributing to Eliza's support.

Thus Freddy and Eliza, now Mr. and Mrs. Eynsford Hill, would have spent a penniless honeymoon but for a wedding present of £500 from the Colonel to Eliza. It lasted a long time because Freddy did not know how to spend money, never having had any to spend, and Eliza, socially trained by a pair of old bachelors, wore her clothes as long as they held together and looked pretty, without the least regard to their being many months out of fashion. Still, £500 will not last two young people for ever; and they both knew, and Eliza felt as well, that they must shift themselves in the end. She could quarter herself on Wimpole Street because it had come to be her home; but she was quite aware that she ought not to quarter Freddy there, and that it would not be good for his character if she did.

Not that the Wimpole Street bachelors objected. When she consulted them, Higgins declined to be bothered about her housing problem when that solution was so simple. Eliza's desire to have Freddy in the house with her seemed of no more importance than if she had wanted an extra piece of bedroom furniture. Pleas as to Freddy's character, and the moral obligation on him to earn his own living, were lost on Higgins. He denied that Freddy had any character, and declared that if he tried to do any useful work some competent person would have the trouble of undoing it: a procedure involving a net loss to the community, and great unhappiness to Freddy himself, who was obviously intended by Nature for such light work as amusing Eliza, which, Higgins declared, was a much more useful and honorable occupation than working in the city. When Eliza referred again to her project of teaching phonetics, Higgins abated not a jot of his violent opposition to it. He said she was not within ten years of being qualified to meddle with his pet subject; and as it was evident that the Colonel agreed with him, she felt she could not go against them in this grave matter, and that she had no right, without Higgins's consent, to exploit the knowledge he had given her; for his knowledge seemed to her as much his private property as his watch: Eliza was no communist. Besides, she was superstitiously devoted to them both, more entirely and frankly after her marriage than before it.

It was the Colonel who finally solved the problem, which had cost him much perplexed cogitation. He one day asked Eliza, rather shyly, whether she had quite given up her notion of keeping a flower shop. She replied that she had thought of it, but had put it out of her head, because the Colonel had said, that day at Mrs. Higgins's, that it would never do. The Colonel confessed that when he said that, he had not quite recovered from the dazzling impression of the day before. They broke the matter to Higgins that evening. The sole comment vouchsafed by him very nearly led to a serious quarrel with Eliza. It was to the effect that she would have in Freddy an ideal errand boy.

Freddy himself was next sounded on the subject. He said he had been thinking of a shop himself; though it had presented itself to his pennilessness as a small place in which Eliza should sell tobacco at one counter whilst he sold newspapers at the opposite one. But he agreed that it would be extraordinarily jolly to go early every morning with Eliza to Covent Garden and buy flowers on the scene of their first meeting: a sentiment which earned him many kisses from his wife. He added that he had always been afraid to propose anything of the sort, because Clara would make an awful row about a step that must damage her matrimonial chances, and his mother could not be expected to like it after clinging for so many years to that step of the social ladder on which retail trade is impossible.

This difficulty was removed by an event highly unexpected by Freddy's mother. Clara, in the course of her incursions into those artistic circles which were the highest within her reach, discovered that her conversational qualifications were expected to include a grounding in the novels of Mr. H. G. Wells. She borrowed them in various directions so energetically that she swallowed them all within two months. The result was a conversion of a kind quite common today. A modern Acts of the Apostles would fill fifty whole Bibles if anyone were capable of writing it.

Poor Clara, who appeared to Higgins and his mother as a disagreeable and ridiculous person, and to her own mother as in some inexplicable way a social failure, had never seen herself in either light; for, though to some extent ridiculed and mimicked in West Kensington like everybody else there, she was accepted as a rational and normal—or shall we say inevitable?—sort of human being. At worst they called her The Pusher; but to them no more than to herself had it ever occurred that she was pushing the air, and pushing it in a wrong direction. Still, she was not happy. She was growing desperate. Her one asset, the fact that her mother was what the Epsom greengrocer called a carriage lady, had no exchange value, apparently. It had prevented her from getting educated, because the only education she could have afforded was education with the Earlscourt greengrocer's daughter. It had led her to seek the society of her mother's class; and that class simply would not have her, because she was much poorer than the greengrocer, and, far from being able to afford a maid, could not afford even a housemaid, and had to scrape along at home with an illiberally treated general servant. Under such circumstances nothing could give her an air of being a genuine product of Largelady Park. And yet its tradition made her regard a marriage with anyone within her reach as an unbearable humiliation. Commercial people and professional people in a small way were odious to her. She ran after painters and novelists; but she did not charm them; and her bold attempts to pick up and practise artistic and literary talk irritated them. She was, in short, an utter failure, an ignorant, incompetent, pretentious, unwelcome, penniless, useless little snob; and though she did not admit these disqualifications (for nobody ever faces unpleasant truths of this kind until the possibility of a way out dawns on them) she felt their effects too keenly to be satisfied with her position.

Clara had a startling eyeopener when, on being suddenly wakened to enthusiasm by a girl of her own age who dazzled her and produced in her a gushing desire to take her for a model, and gain her friendship, she discovered that this exquisite apparition had graduated from the gutter in a few months time. It shook her so violently, that when Mr. H. G. Wells lifted her on the point of his puissant pen, and placed her at the angle of view from which the life she was leading and the society to which she clung appeared in its true relation to real human needs and worthy social structure, he effected a conversion and a conviction of sin comparable to the most sensational feats of General Booth or Gypsy Smith. Clara's snobbery went bang. Life suddenly began to move with her. Without knowing how or why, she began to make friends and enemies. Some of the acquaintances to whom she had been a tedious or indifferent or ridiculous affliction, dropped her: others became cordial. To her amazement she found that some "quite nice" people were saturated with Wells, and that this accessibility to ideas was the secret of their niceness. People she had thought deeply religious and had tried to conciliate on that tack with disastrous results, suddenly took an interest in her, and revealed a hostility to conventional religion which she had never conceived possible except among the most desperate characters. They made her read Galsworthy; and Galsworthy exposed the vanity of Largelady Park and finished her. It exasperated her to think that the dungeon in which she had languished for so many unhappy years had been unlocked all the time, and that the impulses she had so carefully struggled with and stifled for the sake of keeping well with society, were precisely those by which alone she could have come into any sort of sincere human contact. In the radiance of these discoveries, and the tumult of their reaction, she made a fool of herself as freely and conspicuously as when she so rashly adopted Eliza's expletive in Mrs. Higgins's drawing room; for the new-born Wellsian had to find her bearings almost as ridiculously as a baby; but nobody hates a baby for its ineptitudes, or thinks the worse of it for trying to eat the matches; and Clara lost no friends by her follies. They laughed at her to her face this time; and she had to defend herself and fight it out as best she could.

When Freddy paid a visit to Earlscourt (which he never did when he could possibly help it) to make the desolating announcement that he and his Eliza were thinking of blackening the Largelady scutcheon by opening a shop, he found the little household already convulsed by a prior announcement from Clara that she also was going to work in an old furniture shop in Dover Street, which had been started by a fellow Wellsian. This appointment Clara owed, after all, to her old social accomplishment of Push. She had made up her mind that, cost what it might, she would see Mr. Wells in the flesh; and she had achieved her end at a garden party. She had better luck than so rash an enterprise deserved. Mr. Wells came up to her expectations. Age had not withered him, nor could custom stale his infinite variety in half an hour. His pleasant neatness and compactness, his small hands and feet, his teeming ready brain, his unaffected accessibility, and a certain fine apprehensiveness which stamped him as susceptible from his topmost hair to his tipmost toe, proved irresistible. Clara talked of nothing else for weeks and weeks afterwards. And as she happened to talk to the lady of the furniture shop, and that lady also desired above all things to know Mr. Wells and sell pretty things to him, she offered Clara a job on the chance of achieving that end through her.

And so it came about that Eliza's luck held, and the expected opposition to the flower shop melted away. The shop is in the arcade of a railway station not very far from the Victoria and Albert Museum; and if you live in that neighborhood you may go there any day and buy a buttonhole from Eliza.

Now here is a last opportunity for romance. Would you not like to be assured that the shop was an immense success, thanks to Eliza's charms and her early business experience in Covent Garden? Alas! the truth is the truth: the shop did not pay for a long time, simply because Eliza and her Freddy did not know how to keep it. True, Eliza had not to begin at the very beginning: she knew the names and prices of the cheaper flowers; and her elation was unbounded when she found that Freddy, like all youths educated at cheap, pretentious, and thoroughly inefficient schools, knew a little Latin. It was very little, but enough to make him appear to her a Porson or Bentley, and to put him at his ease with botanical nomenclature. Unfortunately he knew nothing else; and Eliza, though she could count money up to eighteen shillings or so, and had acquired a certain familiarity with the language of Milton from her struggles to qualify herself for winning Higgins's bet, could not write out a bill without utterly disgracing the establishment. Freddy's power of stating in Latin that Balbus built a wall and that Gaul was divided into three parts did not carry with it the slightest knowledge of accounts or business: Colonel Pickering had to explain to him what a cheque book and a bank account meant. And the pair were by no means easily teachable. Freddy backed up Eliza in her obstinate refusal to believe that they could save money by engaging a bookkeeper with some knowledge of the business. How, they argued, could you possibly save money by going to extra expense when you already could not make both ends meet? But the Colonel, after making the ends meet over and over again, at last gently insisted; and Eliza, humbled to the dust by having to beg from him so often, and stung by the uproarious derision of Higgins, to whom the notion of Freddy succeeding at anything was a joke that never palled, grasped the fact that business, like phonetics, has to be learned.

On the piteous spectacle of the pair spending their evenings in shorthand schools and polytechnic classes, learning bookkeeping and typewriting with incipient junior clerks, male and female, from the elementary schools, let me not dwell. There were even classes at the London School of Economics, and a humble personal appeal to the director of that institution to recommend a course bearing on the flower business. He, being a humorist, explained to them the method of the celebrated Dickensian essay on Chinese Metaphysics by the gentleman who read an article on China and an article on Metaphysics and combined the information. He suggested that they should combine the London School with Kew Gardens. Eliza, to whom the procedure of the Dickensian gentleman seemed perfectly correct (as in fact it was) and not in the least funny (which was only her ignorance), took the advice with entire gravity. But the effort that cost her the deepest humiliation was a request to Higgins, whose pet artistic fancy, next to Milton's verse, was calligraphy, and who himself wrote a most beautiful Italian hand, that he would teach her to write. He declared that she was congenitally incapable of forming a single letter worthy of the least of Milton's words; but she persisted; and again he suddenly threw himself into the task of teaching her with a combination of stormy intensity, concentrated patience, and occasional bursts of interesting disquisition on the beauty and nobility, the august mission and destiny, of human handwriting. Eliza ended by acquiring an extremely uncommercial script which was a positive extension of her personal beauty, and spending three times as much on stationery as anyone else because certain qualities and shapes of paper became indispensable to her. She could not even address an envelope in the usual way because it made the margins all wrong.

Their commercial schooldays were a period of disgrace and despair for the young couple. They seemed to be learning nothing about flower shops. At last they gave it up as hopeless, and shook the dust of the shorthand schools, and the polytechnics, and the London School of Economics from their feet for ever. Besides, the business was in some mysterious way beginning to take care of itself. They had somehow forgotten their objections to employing other people. They came to the conclusion that their own way was the best, and that they had really a remarkable talent for business. The Colonel, who had been compelled for some years to keep a sufficient sum on current account at his bankers to make up their deficits, found that the provision was unnecessary: the young people were prospering. It is true that there was not quite fair play between them and their competitors in trade. Their week-ends in the country cost them nothing, and saved them the price of their Sunday dinners; for the motor car was the Colonel's; and he and Higgins paid the hotel bills. Mr. F. Hill, florist and greengrocer (they soon discovered that there was money in asparagus; and asparagus led to other vegetables), had an air which stamped the business as classy; and in private life he was still Frederick Eynsford Hill, Esquire. Not that there was any swank about him: nobody but Eliza knew that he had been christened Frederick Challoner. Eliza herself swanked like anything.

That is all. That is how it has turned out. It is astonishing how much Eliza still manages to meddle in the housekeeping at Wimpole Street in spite of the shop and her own family. And it is notable that though she never nags her husband, and frankly loves the Colonel as if she were his favorite daughter, she has never got out of the habit of nagging Higgins that was established on the fatal night when she won his bet for him. She snaps his head off on the faintest provocation, or on none. He no longer dares to tease her by assuming an abysmal inferiority of Freddy's mind to his own. He storms and bullies and derides; but she stands up to him so ruthlessly that the Colonel has to ask her from time to time to be kinder to Higgins; and it is the only request of his that brings a mulish expression into her face. Nothing but some emergency or calamity great enough to break down all likes and dislikes, and throw them both back on their common humanity—and may they be spared any such trial!—will ever alter this. She knows that Higgins does not need her, just as her father did not need her. The very scrupulousness with which he told her that day that he had become used to having her there, and dependent on her for all sorts of little services, and that he should miss her if she went away (it would never have occurred to Freddy or the Colonel to say anything of the sort) deepens her inner certainty that she is "no more to him than them slippers"; yet she has a sense, too, that his indifference is deeper than the infatuation of commoner souls. She is immensely interested in him. She has even secret mischievous moments in which she wishes she could get him alone, on a desert island, away from all ties and with nobody else in the world to consider, and just drag him off his pedestal and see him making love like any common man. We all have private imaginations of that sort. But when it comes to business, to the life that she really leads as distinguished from the life of dreams and fancies, she likes Freddy and she likes the Colonel; and she does not like Higgins and Mr. Doolittle. Galatea never does quite like Pygmalion: his relation to her is too godlike to be altogether agreeable.

RELATED READINGS

Continued

The Story of Pygmalion

from The Metamorphoses

by Ovid
translated by Rolfe Humphries

*Although Henry Higgins keeps insisting that his
interest in Eliza is purely professional, by the
end of the play he admits that he has grown
fond of her. Shaw named his play after a Greek
myth about a sculptor, Pygmalion, who falls in
love with a statue he creates. The following
version of the story was written early in the
first century by Ovid, a Roman poet whose
witty and sophisticated love poems have been
an important source for many writers, including
Shakespeare.*

One man, Pygmalion, who had seen these women
Leading their shameful lives, shocked at the vices
Nature has given the female disposition
Only too often, chose to live alone,
5   To have no woman in his bed. But meanwhile
He made, with marvelous art, an ivory statue,
As white as snow, and gave it greater beauty
Than any girl could have, and fell in love
With his own workmanship. The image seemed
10   That of a virgin, truly, almost living,
And willing, save that modesty prevented,
To take on movement. The best art, they say,
Is that which conceals art, and so Pygmalion

Marvels, and loves the body he has fashioned.
15   He would often move his hands to test and touch it,
Could this be flesh, or was it ivory only?
No, it could not be ivory. His kisses,
He fancies, she returns; he speaks to her,
Holds her, believes his fingers almost leave
20   An imprint on her limbs, and fears to bruise her.
He pays her compliments, and brings her presents
Such as girls love, smooth pebbles, winding shells,
Little pet birds, flowers with a thousand colors,
Lilies, and painted balls, and lumps of amber.
25   He decks her limbs with dresses, and her fingers
Wear rings which he puts on, and he brings a necklace,
And earrings, and a ribbon for her bosom,
And all of these become her, but she seems
Even more lovely naked, and he spreads
30   A crimson coverlet for her to lie on,
Takes her to bed, puts a soft pillow under
Her head, as if she felt it, calls her *Darling,*
My darling love!
                "And Venus' holiday
35   Came round, and all the people of the island
Were holding festival, and snow-white heifers,
Their horns all tipped with gold, stood at the altars,
Where incense burned, and, timidly, Pygmalion
Made offering, and prayed: 'If you can give
40   All things, O gods, I pray my wife may be—
(He almost said, *My ivory girl,* but dared not)—
One like my ivory girl.' And golden Venus
Was there, and understood the prayer's intention,
And showed her presence, with the bright flame leaping
45   Thrice on the altar, and Pygmalion came
Back where the maiden lay, and lay beside her,
And kissed her, and she seemed to glow, and kissed her,
And stroked her breast, and felt the ivory soften
Under his fingers, as wax grows soft in sunshine,

50 Made pliable by handling. And Pygmalion
Wonders, and doubts, is dubious and happy,
Plays lover again, and over and over touches
The body with his hand. It is a body!
The veins throb under the thumb. And oh, Pygmalion
55 Is lavish in his prayer and praise to Venus,
No words are good enough. The lips he kisses
Are real indeed, the ivory girl can feel them,
And blushes and responds, and the eyes open
At once on lover and heaven, and Venus blesses
60 The marriage she has made. The crescent moon
Fills to full orb, nine times, and wanes again,
And then a daughter is born, a girl named Paphos,
From whom the island later takes its name.

Excerpt from My Fair Lady

by Alan Jay Lerner

One of the most famous lines spoken by Eliza Doolittle doesn't even appear in Pygmalion! *The scene where Higgins makes Eliza recite "The rain in Spain stays mainly in the plain" actually comes from the following musical version of the play. In addition to its memorable songs,* My Fair Lady *provides a glimpse of certain events that Shaw chose not to dramatize, such as the grueling language training Eliza undergoes with Higgins.*

(*The lights come up in the study.* Eliza *is on the stool in front of the desk.* Higgins *is in the alcove repairing a metronome.* Pickering *as usual is in the wing chair reading the London* Times.)

Eliza. The rine in spine sties minely in the pline.

Higgins (*correcting her*). The rain in Spain stays mainly in the plain.

Eliza. Didn't I sy that?

Higgins. No, Eliza, you didn't "sy" that. You didn't even "say" that. (*He picks up a small burner and brings it down to the desk.*) Every night before you get into bed, where you used to say your prayers, I want you to repeat: "The rain in Spain stays mainly in the plain," fifty times. You will get much further with the Lord if you learn not to offend His ears. Now for your "H's." Pickering, this is going to be ghastly!

Pickering. Control yourself, Higgins. Give the girl a chance.

Higgins (*patiently*). Of course. No one expects her to get it right the first time. Watch closely, Eliza. (*He places the burner on the desk and lights the flame.*) You see this flame? Every time you say your aitch properly, the flame will waver. Every time you drop your aitch, the flame will remain stationary. That's how you will know you've done it correctly; in time your ear will hear the difference. Now, listen carefully; in Hertford, Hereford and Hampshire, hurricanes hardly ever happen.

(Eliza *sits down behind the desk.*)

Now repeat after me, In Hertford, Hereford and Hampshire, hurricanes hardly even happen.

Eliza (*conscientiously*). In 'ertford, 'ereford and 'ampshire, 'urricanes 'ahdly hever 'appen!

Higgins (*infuriated*). No, no, no, no! Have you no ear at all?

Eliza (*willingly*). Should I do it over?

Higgins. No. Please, no! We must start from the very beginning. (*He kneels before the flame.*) Do this: ha, ha, ha, ha. (*He rises.*)

Eliza. Ha—ha—ha—ha. (*She looks up at him happily.*)

Higgins. Well, go on. Go on.

(Eliza *continues.* Higgins *strolls casually over to* Pickering, *leaving* Eliza *to aspirate at the flame.*)

Does the same thing hold true in India, Pickering; the peculiar habit of not only dropping a letter like the letter aitch, but using it where it shouldn't be? Like "hever" instead of "ever"? You'll notice some of the Slavic peoples when they learn to speak English have a tendency to that with their G's. They say "linger" (soft g) instead of "linger" (hard g); and then they turn around and say "singer" (hard g) instead of "singer" (soft g).

(Pickering *had never thought about it and naturally is perplexed.*)

I wonder why that's so. I must look it up.

(Higgins *starts for the landing.* Eliza, *by this time, is sinking fast from lack of oxygen.* Pickering *notices her dying gasps and pulls* Higgins' *arm to call his attention to it.*)

(*Thinking which book to consult*)

Go on! Go on!

(*He continues up the stairs.* Eliza *musters together one final "HA" and blows out the flame. The room is plunged into darkness.*)

(*In the darkness, six* Servants *emerge, and stand in a spotlight at the far end of the study.*)

Servants.
>Poor Professor Higgins!
>Poor Professor Higgins!
>Night and day
>He slaves away!
>Oh, poor Professor Higgins!
>All day long
>On his feet;
>Up and down until he's numb;
>Doesn't rest;
>Doesn't eat;
>Doesn't touch a crumb!

(*The spotlight goes off. The* Servants *disappear and the lights come up in the study.* Pickering *is seated in his favorite*

chair with a large and fulsome tea table before him. Eliza is
on the sofa. Higgins is standing by the xylophone, a cup in
one hand, a xylophone mallet in the other. He taps out eight
notes. "How kind of you to let me come.")

Higgins. *Kind* of you, *kind* of you, *kind* of you. Now
listen, Eliza. (*He plays them again.*) How kind of you
to let me come.

Eliza. How kind of *you* to let me come.

Higgins (*puts down the mallet in despair and walks over to
the tea table*). No! *Kind* of you. It's just like "*cup* of
tea." *Kind* of you—*cup* of tea. *Kind* of you—Say
"cup of tea."

Eliza (*hungrily*). Cappatea.

Higgins. No! No! A cup of tea . . . (*Takes a mouthful of
cake from the tray*) It's awfully good cake. I wonder
where Mrs. Pearce gets it?

Pickering. Mmmmm! First rate! The strawberry tarts
are delicious. And did you try the pline cake?
(Higgins *looks at him in horror and then turns to* Eliza.)

Higgins. Now, try it again, Eliza. A cup of tea. A cup
of tea.

Eliza (*longingly*). A cappatea.

Higgins. Can't you hear the difference? Put your
tongue forward until it squeezes against the top of
your lower teeth. Now say "cup."

Eliza (*her attention only on the cake in* Higgins' *hand*).
C-cup.

Higgins. Now say "of."

Eliza. Of.

Higgins. Now say, cup, cup, cup, cup—of, of, of, of.

Eliza. Cup, cup, cup, cup—of, of, of, of! Cup, cup, cup, cup—of, of, of, of . . .

Pickering (*as she's practicing*). By Jove, that was a glorious tea, Higgins. Do finish the strawberry tart. I couldn't eat another thing.

Higgins. No, thanks, old chap, really.

Pickering. It's a shame to waste it.

Higgins. Oh, it won't go to waste. (*He takes the last tart*) I know someone who's immensely fond of strawberry tarts.

(*Eliza's eyes light up hopefully. But alas,* Higgins *walks right past her and goes to the bird cage.*)

Higgins (*pushing the cake thru the bars*). Cheep, cheep, cheep!

Eliza (*shrieking*). Aaaaaaaaaaaoooooooooowwww!!

Blackout

(*The lights black out and the* Servants *again appear in the spotlight*)

Servants.
      Poor Professor Higgins!
      Poor Professor Higgins!
      On he plods
      Against all odds;
      Oh, poor Professor Higgins!
      Nine P.M.
      Ten P.M.
      On through midnight ev'ry night.
      One A.M.
      Two A.M.
      Three . . .!

(The spotlight goes off. The Servants *disappear and the lights come up again in the study.* Eliza *is seated in the wing chair.* Higgins *has drawn up the stool and is facing her, a small box of marbles in his hand. He is placing them in her mouth.)*

Higgins. Four . . . five . . . six marbles. There we are. *(He holds up a slip of paper.)* Now, I want you to read this and enunciate each word just as if the marbles were not in your mouth. "With blackest moss, the flower pots were thickly crusted, one and all." Each word clear as a bell. *(He gives her the paper.)*

Eliza *(unintelligibly).* With blackest moss the flower pots . . . I can't! I can't!

Pickering *(from the sofa).* I say, Higgins, are those pebbles really necessary?

Higgins. If they were necessary for Demosthenes, they are necessary for Eliza Doolittle. Go on, Eliza.

Eliza *(trying again with no better results).* With blackest moss, the flower pots were thickly crusted, one and all. . . .

Higgins. I cannot understand a word. Not a word.

Eliza *(her anger coming thru the marbles and "flowerpots").* With blackest moss, the flowerpots were thickly crusted, one and all; the rusted nails fell from the knots that held the pear to the gable-wall . . .

Pickering *(soon after she has begun).* I say, Higgins, perhaps the poem is too difficult for the girl. Why don't you try a simpler one, like: "The Owl and the Pussycat"? Oh, yes, that's a charming one.

Higgins *(bellowing).* Pickering! I cannot hear the girl!

(Eliza gasps and takes the marbles out of her mouth.)

Excerpt from *My Fair Lady*   159

What's the matter? Why did you stop?

Eliza. I swallowed one.

Higgins (*reassuringly*). Oh, don't worry. I have plenty more. Open your mouth.

(*The lights go out and into the spotlight again appear the Servants.*)

Servants.
> Quit, Professor Higgins!
> Quit, Professor Higgins!
> Hear our plea
> Or payday we
> Will quit, Professor Higgins!
> Ay not I,
> O not Ow,
> Pounding, pounding in our brain.
> Ay not I,
> O, not Ow,
> Don't say "Rine," say "Rain" . . .

(*The spotlight goes off. The Servants disappear and the lights come up again on the study. Eliza is draped wearily on the sofa. Pickering is half asleep in the wing chair. Higgins is seated at his desk, an ice-bag on his head. The gray light outside the windows indicates the early hours of the morning.*)

Higgins (*wearily*). The rain in Spain stays mainly in the plain.

Eliza. I can't. I'm so tired. I'm so tired.

Pickering (*half asleep*). Oh, for heaven's sake, Higgins. It must be three o'clock in the morning. Do be reasonable.

Higgins (*rising*). I am always reasonable. Eliza, if I can go on with a blistering headache, you can.

Eliza. I have a headache, too.

Higgins. Here.

(*He plops the ice-bag on her head. She takes it off her head and buries her face in her hands, exhausted to the point of tears.*)

(*With sudden gentleness*) Eliza, I know you're tired. I know your head aches. I know your nerves are as raw as meat in a butcher's window. But think what you're trying to accomplish. (*He sits next to her on sofa*) Think what you're dealing with. The majesty and grandeur of the English language. It's the greatest possession we have. The noblest sentiments that ever flowed in the hearts of men are contained in its extraordinary, imaginative and musical mixtures of sounds. That's what you've set yourself to conquer, Eliza. And conquer it you will. (*He rises, goes to the chair behind his desk and seats himself heavily.*) Now, try it again.

Eliza (*slowly*). The rain in Spain stays mainly in the plain.

Higgins (*sitting up*). What was that?

Eliza. The rain in Spain stays mainly in the plain.

Higgins (*rising, unbelievably*). Again.

Eliza. The rain in Spain stays mainly in the plain.

Higgins (*to Pickering*). I think she's got it! I think she's got it!

Eliza. The rain in Spain stays mainly in the plain.

Higgins (*triumphantly*).

> By George, she's got it!
> By George, she's got it!

Now once again, where does it rain?

Eliza. On the plain! On the plain!

Higgins. And where's that soggy plain?

Eliza. In Spain! In Spain!

(Pickering *jumps to his feet and the three sing out joyously.*)

The three.

> The rain in Spain stays mainly in the plain!
> The rain in Spain stays mainly in the plain!

(Higgins *walks excitedly to the xylophone.*)

Higgins. In Hertford, Hereford and Hampshire . . . ?

Eliza. Hurricanes hardly happen.

Higgins (*taps out "How kind of you to let me come"*).

Eliza. How kind of you to let me come!

Higgins (*putting down the mallet and turning back to her*).

Now once again, where does it rain?

Eliza. On the plain! On the plain!

Higgins. And where's that blasted plain?

Eliza. In Spain! In Spain!

The three.

> The rain in Spain stays mainly in the plain!
> The rain in Spain stays mainly in the plain!

(*Joy and victory!* Higgins *takes a handkerchief from his pocket and waves it in front of* Pickering *who charges it like the finest bull in Spain.* Higgins *turns and grabs* Eliza *and*

(they do a few awkward tango steps while Pickering *jumps around like a flamenco dancer shouting "Viva Higgins, Viva." Higgins swings Eliza onto the sofa and joins Pickering in a bit of heel-clicking. Eliza jumps down from the sofa. They throw themselves into a wild jig and then all collapse back upon the sofa engulfed in laughter.)*

(Mrs. Pearce *enters in her nightrobe, followed by two of the* Servants *who have also been awakened.)*

Higgins. Pickering, we're making fine progress. I think the time has come to try her out.

Mrs. Pearce (*making her presence known*). Are you feeling all right, Mr. Higgins?

Higgins. Quite well, thank you, Mrs. Pearce. And you?

Mrs. Pearce. Very well, sir, thank you.

Higgins. Splendid. (*To* Pickering) Let's test her in public and see how she fares.

Mrs. Pearce. Mr. Higgins, I was awakened by a dreadful pounding. Do you know what it might have been?

Higgins. Pounding? I heard no pounding. Did you, Pickering?

Pickering (*innocently*). No.

Higgins. If this continues, Mrs. Pearce, I should see a doctor. Pickering, I know! Let's take her to the races.

Pickering (*rising*). The races!?

Higgins (*rising too, excited by the idea*). Yes! My mother's box at Ascot.

Pickering (*cautiously*). You'll consult your mother first, of course.

Higgins. Of course. (*Thinking better of it*) No! We'll surprise her. Let's go straight to bed. First thing in the morning we'll go off and buy her a dress. Eliza, go on with your work.

Mrs. Pearce. But Mr. Higgins, it's early in the morning!

Higgins. What better time to work than early in the morning? (*To* Pickering) Where does one buy a lady's gown?

Pickering. Whiteley's, of course.

Higgins. How do you know that?

Pickering. Common knowledge.

Higgins (*studying* Pickering *carefully*). We mustn't get her anything too flowery. I despise those gowns with a sort of weed here and a weed there. Something simple, modest and elegant is what's called for. Perhaps with a sash. (*He places the imaginary sash on Pickering's hip and steps back to eye it.*) Yes. Just right.

(*He goes out the door.* Pickering *looks down at his hip to reassure himself the sash is not there and follows after him.*)

(Mrs. Pearce, *whose face has been a study in amazement, goes quickly to* Eliza.)

Mrs. Pearce. You've all been working much too hard. I think the strain is beginning to show. Eliza, I don't care what Mr. Higgins says, you must put down your books and go to bed.

Eliza (*lost on an errant cloud only hears her from far below*).

Bed! Bed! I couldn't go to bed!
My head's too light to try to set it down!

Sleep! Sleep! I couldn't sleep tonight!
Not for all the jewels in the crown!

I could have danced all night!
I could have danced all night!
And still have begged for more.
I could have spread my wings
And done a thousand things
I've never done before.

I'll never know
What made it so exciting;
Why all at once
My heart took flight.
I only knew when he
Began to dance with me,
I could have danced, danced, danced all night!

1st Servant (*to* Eliza). It's after three, now.

2nd Servant (*to* Mrs. Pearce).

Don't you agree, now,
She ought to be in bed?

(Mrs. Pearce *nods emphatically.*)

Eliza (*telling the servants*).

I could have danced all night!
I could have danced all night!
And still have begged for more.
I could have spread my wings
And done a thousand things
I've never done before.

Excerpt from *My Fair Lady*   165

Servants (*simultaneously telling* Eliza).

> You're tired out.
> You must be dead.
> Your face is drawn.
> Your eyes are red.
> Now say goodnight, please.
> Turn out the light, please.
> It's really time.
> For you to be in bed.
> Do come along.
> Do as you're told,
> Or Mrs. Pearce
> Is apt to scold.
> You're up too late, miss.
> And sure as fate, miss.
> You'll catch a cold.

(Mrs. Pearce *goes to the alcove for a comforter.*)

Eliza.

> I'll never know
> What made it so exciting,
> Why all at once
> My heart took flight.
> I only know when he
> Began to dance with me
> I could have danced, danced, danced all night!

Servants (*simultaneously*).

> Put down your book
> The work'll keep.
> Now settle down
> And go to sleep.

(Eliza *stretches out on the sofa and* Mrs. Pearce *covers her with a comforter.*)

Mrs. Pearce.

> I understand, dear.
> It's all been grand, dear.
> But now it's time to sleep.

(*She turns out the lights and she and the* Servants *go.*)

Eliza (*reliving it*).

> I could have danced all night!
> I could have danced all night!
> And still have begged for more.
> I could have spread my wings,
> And done a thousand things
> I've never done before.
> I'll never know
> What made it so exciting,
> Why all at once
> My heart took flight.

(*She throws off the comforter and jumps to her feet.*)

> I only know when he
> Began to dance with me
> I could have danced, danced, danced all night!

Her First Ball

by Katherine Mansfield

After Eliza's great success in polite society, Higgins and Pickering continue to treat her the same as before. Why did she expect her life to be transformed by this one evening? In the following story, we get a hint of the emotions and sensations Eliza might have experienced at the grand reception.

Exactly when the ball began Leila would have found it hard to say. Perhaps her first real partner was the cab. It did not matter that she shared the cab with the Sheridan girls and their brother. She sat back in her own little corner of it, and the bolster on which her hand rested felt like the sleeve of an unknown young man's dress suit; and away they bowled, past waltzing lamp-posts and houses and fences and trees.

"Have you really never been to a ball before, Leila? But, my child, how too weird—" cried the Sheridan girls.

"Our nearest neighbour was fifteen miles," said Leila softly, gently opening and shutting her fan.

Oh, dear, how hard it was to be indifferent like the others! She tried not to smile too much; she tried not to care. But every single thing was so new and exciting . . . Meg's tuberoses, Jose's long loop of amber, Laura's little dark head, pushing above her white fur like a flower through snow. She would remember for ever. It even gave her a pang to see her cousin Laurie throw away the wisps of tissue paper he pulled from the fastenings of his new gloves. She would like to have kept those wisps as a keepsake, as a remembrance.

Laurie leaned forward and put his hand on Laura's knee.

"Look here, darling," he said. "The third and the ninth as usual. Twig?"

Oh, how marvellous to have a brother! In her excitement Leila felt that if there had been time, if it hadn't been impossible, she couldn't have helped crying because she was an only child, and no brother had ever said "Twig?" to her; no sister would ever say, as Meg said to Jose that moment, "I've never known your hair go up more successfully than it has to-night!"

But, of course, there was no time. They were at the drill hall already; there were cabs in front of them and cabs behind. The road was bright on either side with moving fan-like lights, and on the pavement gay couples seemed to float through the air; little satin shoes chased each other like birds.

"Hold on to me, Leila; you'll get lost," said Laura.

"Come on, girls, let's make a dash for it," said Laurie.

Leila put two fingers on Laura's pink velvet cloak, and they were somehow lifted past the big golden lantern, carried along the passage, and pushed into the little room marked "Ladies." Here the crowd was so great there was hardly space to take off their things; the noise was deafening. Two benches on either side were stacked high with wraps. Two old women in white aprons ran up and down tossing fresh armfuls. And everybody was pressing forward trying to get at the little dressing-table and mirror at the far end.

A great quivering jet of gas lighted the ladies' room. It couldn't wait; it was dancing already. When the door opened again and there came a burst of tuning from the drill hall, it leaped almost to the ceiling.

Dark girls, fair girls were patting their hair, tying ribbons again, tucking handkerchiefs down the fronts of their bodices, smoothing marble-white gloves. And because they were all laughing it seemed to Leila that they were all lovely.

"Aren't there any invisible hair-pins?" cried a voice. "How most extrordinary! I can't see a single invisible hair-pin."

"Powder my back, there's a darling," cried some one else.

"But I must have a needle and cotton. I've torn simply miles and miles of the frill," wailed a third.

Then, "Pass them along, pass them along!" The straw basket of programmes was tossed from arm to arm. Darling little pink-and-silver programmes, with pink pencils and fluffy tassels. Leila's fingers shook as she took one out of the basket. She wanted to ask some one, "Am I meant to have one too?" but she had just time to read: "Waltz 3. *Two, Two in a Canoe.* Polka 4. *Making the Feathers Fly*," when Meg cried, "Ready, Leila?" and they pressed their way through the crush in the passage towards the big double doors of the drill hall.

Dancing had not begun yet, but the band had stopped tuning, and the noise was so great it seemed that when it did begin to play it would never be heard. Leila, pressing close to Meg, looking over Meg's shoulder, felt that even the little quivering coloured flags strung across the ceiling were talking. She quite forgot to be shy; she forgot how in the middle of dressing she had sat down on the bed with one shoe off and one shoe on and begged her mother to ring up her cousins and say she couldn't go after all. And the rush of longing she had had to be sitting on the veranda of their forsaken up-country home, listening to the baby owls crying "More pork" in the moonlight, was changed to a rush of joy so sweet that it was hard to bear alone. She clutched her fan, and, gazing at the gleaming, golden floor, the azaleas, the lanterns, the stage at one end with its red carpet and gilt chairs and the band in a corner, she thought breathlessly, "How heavenly; how simply heavenly!"

All the girls stood grouped together at one side of the doors, the men at the other, and the chaperones in dark dresses, smiling rather foolishly, walked with little careful steps over the polished floor towards the stage.

"This is my little country cousin Leila. Be nice to her. Find her partners; she's under my wing," said Meg, going up to one girl after another.

Strange faces smiled at Leila—sweetly, vaguely. Strange voices answered, "Of course, my dear." But Leila felt the girls didn't really see her. They were looking towards the men. Why didn't the men begin? What were they waiting for? There they stood, smoothing their gloves, patting their glossy hair and smiling among themselves. Then, quite suddenly, as if they had only just made up their minds that that was what they had to do, the men came gliding over the parquet. There was a joyful flutter among the girls. A tall, fair man flew up to Meg, seized her programme, scribbled something; Meg passed him on to Leila. "May I have the pleasure?" He ducked and smiled. There came a dark man wearing an eyeglass, then cousin Laurie with a friend, and Laura with a little freckled fellow whose tie was crooked. Then quite an old man—fat, with a big bald patch on his head— took her programme and murmured, "Let me see, let me see!" And he was a long time comparing his programme, which looked black with names, with hers. It seemed to give him so much trouble that Leila was ashamed. "Oh, please don't bother," she said eagerly. But instead of replying the fat man wrote something, glanced at her again. "Do I remember this bright little face?" he said softly. "Is it known to me of yore?" At that moment the band began playing; the fat man disappeared. He was tossed away on a great wave of music that came flying over the gleaming floor, breaking the groups up into couples, scattering them, sending them spinning. . . .

Leila had learned to dance at boarding school. Every Saturday afternoon the boarders were hurried off to a little corrugated iron mission hall where Miss Eccles (of London) held her "select" classes. But the difference between that dusty-smelling hall—with calico texts on the walls, the poor terrified little woman in a brown velvet toque with rabbit's ears thumping the cold piano, Miss Eccles poking the girls' feet with her long white wand—and this was so tremendous that Leila was sure if her partner didn't come and she had to listen to that marvellous music and to watch the others sliding, gliding over the golden floor, she would die at least, or faint, or lift her arms and fly out of one of those dark windows that showed the stars.

"Ours, I think—" Some one bowed, smiled, and offered her his arm; she hadn't to die after all. Some one's hand pressed her waist, and she floated away like a flower that is tossed into a pool.

"Quite a good floor, isn't it?" drawled a faint voice close to her ear.

"I think it's most beautifully slippery," said Leila.

"Pardon!" The faint voice sounded surprised. Leila said it again. And there was a tiny pause before the voice echoed, "Oh, quite!" and she was swung round again.

He steered so beautifully. That was the great difference between dancing with girls and men, Leila decided. Girls banged into each other, and stamped on each other's feet; the girl who was gentleman always clutched you so.

The azaleas were separate flowers no longer; they were pink and white flags streaming by.

"Were you at the Bells' last week?" the voice came again. It sounded tired. Leila wondered whether she ought to ask him if he would like to stop.

"No, this is my first dance," said she.

Her partner gave a little gasping laugh. "Oh, I say," he protested.

"Yes, it is really the first dance I've ever been to." Leila was most fervent. It was such a relief to be able to tell somebody. "You see, I've lived in the country all my life up until now. . . . "

At that moment the music stopped, and they went to sit on two chairs against the wall. Leila tucked her pink satin feet under and fanned herself, while she blissfully watched the other couples passing and disappearing through the swing doors.

"Enjoying yourself, Leila?" asked Jose, nodding her golden head.

Laura passed and gave her the faintest little wink; it made Leila wonder for a moment whether she was quite grown up after all. Certainly her partner did not say very much. He coughed, tucked his handkerchief away, pulled down his waistcoat, took a minute thread off his sleeve. But it didn't matter. Almost immediately the band started, and her second partner seemed to spring from the ceiling.

"Floor's not bad," said the new voice. Did one always begin with the floor? And then, "Were you at the Neaves' on Tuesday?" And again Leila explained. Perhaps it was a little strange that her partners were not more interested. For it was thrilling. Her first ball! She was only at the beginning of everything. It seemed to her that she had never known what the night was like before. Up till now it had been dark, silent, beautiful very often—oh, yes—but mournful some-how. Solemn. And now it would never be like that again—it had opened dazzling bright.

"Care for an ice?" said her partner. And they went

through the swing doors, down the passage, to the supper room. Her cheeks burned, she was fearfully thirsty. How sweet the ices looked on little glass plates, and how cold the frosted spoon was, iced too! And when they came back to the hall there was the fat man waiting for her by the door. It gave her quite a shock again to see how old he was; he ought to have been on the stage with the fathers and mothers. And when Leila compared him with her other partners he looked shabby. His waistcoat was creased, there was a button off his glove, his coat looked as if it was dusty with French chalk.

"Come along, little lady," said the fat man. He scarcely troubled to clasp her, and they moved away so gently, it was more like walking than dancing. But he said not a word about the floor. "Your first dance, isn't it?" he murmured.

"How *did* you know?"

"Ah," said the fat man, "that's what it is to be old!" He wheezed faintly as he steered her past an awkward couple. "You see, I've been doing this kind of thing for the last thirty years."

"Thirty years?" cried Leila. Twelve years before she was born!

"It hardly bears thinking about, does it?" said the fat man gloomily. Leila looked at his bald head, and she felt quite sorry for him.

"I think it's marvellous to be still going on," she said kindly.

"Kind little lady," said the fat man, and he pressed her a little closer, and hummed a bar of the waltz. "Of course," he said, "you can't hope to last anything like as long as that. No-o," said the fat man, "long before that you'll be sitting up there on the stage, looking on, in your nice black velvet. And these pretty arms will have turned into little short fat ones, and you'll beat time with such a different kind of fan—a black bony one." The fat man seemed to shudder. "And you'll smile away like the poor old dears up there, and point to your daughter, and tell the elderly lady next to you how some dreadful man tried to kiss her at the club ball. And your heart will ache, ache"—the fat man squeezed her closer still, as if he really was sorry for that poor heart—"because no one wants to kiss you now. And you'll say how unpleasant these polished floors are to walk on, how dangerous they are. Eh, Mademoiselle Twinkletoes?" said the fat man softly.

Leila gave a light little laugh, but she did not feel like laughing. Was it—could it all be true? It sounded terribly true. Was this first ball only the beginning of her last ball after all? At that the music seemed to change; it sounded sad, sad; it rose upon a great sigh. Oh, how quickly things changed! Why didn't happiness last for ever? For ever wasn't a bit too long.

"I want to stop," she said in a breathless voice. The fat man led her to the door.

"No," she said, "I won't go outside. I won't sit down. I'll just stand here, thank you." She leaned against the wall, tapping with her foot, pulling up her gloves and trying to smile. But deep inside her a little girl threw her pinafore over her head and sobbed. Why had he spoiled it all?

"I say, you know," said the fat man, "you mustn't take me seriously, little lady."

"As if I should!" said Leila, tossing her small dark head and sucking her underlip. . . .

Again the couples paraded. The swing doors opened and shut. Now new music was given out by the bandmaster. But Leila didn't want to dance any more. She wanted to be home, or sitting on the veranda listening to those baby owls. When she looked through the dark windows at the stars, they had long beams like wings. . . .

But presently a soft, melting, ravishing tune began,

and a young man with curly hair bowed before her. She would have to dance, out of politeness, until she could find Meg. Very stiffly she walked into the middle; very haughtily she put her hand on his sleeve. But in one minute, in one turn, her feet glided, glided. The lights, the azaleas, the dresses, the pink faces, the velvet chairs, all became one beautiful flying wheel. And when her next partner bumped her into the fat man and he said, *"Pardon,"* she smiled at him more radiantly than ever. She didn't even recognize him again.

The London Language

from The Story of English

by Robert McCrum, William Cran, and Robert MacNeil

*Eliza and her father both speak Cockney, a
dialect of English spoken by the working
class residents of London's East End.
Cockney speakers are known for their
exuberant and playful use of language.
Although Cockney is associated with a
small section of London, the dialect has
influenced how English is spoken in places
as far away as Australia. The following
excerpt from a history of the English
language describes how Cockney has
developed over the centuries.*

In 1899, when the British Empire was at its height,
George Bernard Shaw took his first shot at the
pretensions of English speech in *Captain Brassbound's
Conversion*. Although the play has been overs-
hadowed by the later, and more successful,
Pygmalion, it exhibits all Shaw's special fascination
with the class geography of London talk. At the end of
the published text Shaw addresses himself to perhaps
the most famous characteristic of London talk, the
silent or dropped "aitch".

I should say that in England he who bothers about his *h*s is a fool, and he who ridicules a dropped *h* is a snob. As to the interpolated *h*, my experience as a London vestryman has convinced me that it is often effective as a means of emphasis, and that the London language would be poorer without it.

This "London language" has deep historical roots. The word *cockney*—from *coken-ay,* a cock's egg, an inferior or worthless thing—is as old as Chaucer, and the original use of Cockney had little to do with the idea of "bad English". In the sixteenth century, Cockney was simply the language of all Londoners who were not part of the Court, and was spoken by all sorts and conditions of people, craftsmen, clerks, shopkeepers and tradesmen. One of these, a funeral furnisher named Henry Machyn, kept a diary, and it is clear from the spellings he uses that he was talking "the London language". He left *h*s off words because he never heard people pronounce them. So "half" appears as *alffe,* and *Ampton* is Machyn's spelling of "Hampton". Many of his other spellings suggest Cockney: *frust* for "thrust", *farding* for "farthing", and *Fever stone* for "Featherstone". He would also add a *t* to make *orphant* and *sermont.* For the words we know as "chains", "strange" and "obtain", he wrote *chynes, strynge,* and *obtyn.* Henry Machyn's English had its roots in the Anglo-Saxon regions of East Mercia, East Anglia and Kent, the English of Shakespeare's Mistress Quickly, and later of Sam Weller in Pickwick Papers. It was the speech of the working Londoner.

The transformation of Cockney into the working-class speech of East London, and its gradual redefinition as "low", "ugly" or "coarse", occurred in the eighteenth century, the age of Samuel Johnson and "correct English". The same economic forces that created a market for dictionaries and books of etiquette transformed the City into the square mile of money and trade it is today. The old City dwellers—street traders, artisans, and guildworkers—were driven out. They took their distinctive accents to the docklands of Wapping and Shoreditch, and across the river to Bermondsey. They were joined by refugees from the now middle-class West End, as the new Georgian squares and terraces of Bloomsbury and Kensington displaced the working population. At the same time, the gathering momentum of the industrial revolution was depopulating the neighbouring countryside of Essex, Suffolk, Kent and Middlesex, sending tens of thousands of destitute farmworkers to the East End in search of work. These country immigrants now added their speech traditions to "the London language".

The situation of spoken English in London at the end of the eighteenth century was neatly summarized by Thomas Sheridan, whose definition of the Irish brogue and criticisms of Scottish "rusticity" we noted earlier:

> Two different modes of pronunciation prevail, by which the inhabitants of one part of the town are distinguished from those of the other. One is current in the City, and is called the cockney; the other at the court end, and is called the polite pronunciation.

That "polite pronunciation" was now coming much closer to the language the southern English middle class speaks today. In the words of a contemporary lexicographer, Standard English was now based on "the general practice of men of letters and polite speakers in the Metropolis". One of the most distinctive changes was the now widespread lengthening of the vowel in words like *fast* and *path*. The long *a* became, and has remained, one of the distinguishing features of upper- and upper middle-class English speech, the backbone of BBC English, and the inspiration for the famous lyric, "I say tomato and you say tomahto". Another change occurred to words with *oi* like "boiled", "coiled", and "soiled". These previously had been pronounced *biled, kiled,* and *siled,* pronunciations which are now, oddly enough, popularly attributed to the British Royal Family. Words like "certain", "learn", and "merchant", for which the "correct" pronunciation had been *satrin, larn* and *marchant,* lost their characteristic *ar,* with a few anomalous exceptions like *clerk* and *Derby.* The *r* which is such a mark of American speech, continued to weaken. "More" became *maw,* "harbour" became *hahbah,* and so on. And the *r* at the end of a word like *orator* became what the English critic Raymond Williams has called "a mere glide of the voice"—the distinguishing mark of English in the public schools, the imperial Civil Service, and finally the BBC. At the same time, the received idea of a Cockney became steadily more contemptuous. By the turn of the century, writers like Leigh Hunt and William Hazlitt were scornfully referred to as "Cockney Homers and Virgils". John Keats, the ostler's son, was known, at least to *Blackwood's Magazine,* as the "Cockney poet". Such references were social rather than phonetic. A Cockney was merely a lower-class Londoner who spoke the city's language. The speech of East Enders may have been implicitly despised or laughed at, but it was not labelled "Cockney" in the way that it is today.

It was the Education Acts of the late-Victorian years, with their emphasis on "correct English" and the three

Rs, that isolated the speech of the London working class. In the poverty-stricken East End these educational reforms made little impact: the speech of the district remained unreformed. By the turn of the century, it was fast becoming the Cockney of caricature and stereotype. Now we find Shaw, among others, referring to the "Cockney dialect". Only then did Cockney become synonymous with a way of talk as well as with a way of life. The appearance of Eliza Doolittle in *Pygmalion* with her "kerbstone English" of *flars* and *garn* (go on) and *Ay-ee, Ba-yee, Cy-ee* (A, B, C), consummated the marriage of East End and Cockney. . . .

The life of the street was crucial to the making of late-Victorian Cockney. The close-knit rural communities of East Anglia, Kent and Middlesex from which the majority of East Enders came kept their oral traditions alive on the streets, and in the ale houses and wash houses of Limehouse and Stratford East. When the rural poor were crammed together in the slums of the East End many of the conditions in which the oral tradition of the countryside had flourished were intensified. There was no privacy; everything happened on the street; they were isolated in a particular part of London, not least by the twists and turns of the River Thames. The tradition of spoken English lives on to this day, as Bob Barltrop puts it:

> If there's anything that distinguishes the Cockney, it's his sheer enjoyment of words. He loves to stand them on end and make them jump through hoops and turn circles . . . There's nothing better to a Cockney than to talk—to talk enjoyably, to talk colourfully, to use wonderful phrases. That's Cockney.

This love of nuance, rhythm, word-play and innovation is part of the explanation for the persistent rule-breaking in some elements of Cockney grammar. Some phrases simply *sound* better when the grammar (strictly speaking) is wrong. "That ain't got nothing to do with it" is much more emphatic than the Standard English "That has nothing to do with it".

What does Cockney sound like? Undoubtedly, it has changed since its Victorian days. Then it was, apparently, thinner and reedier in sound. Older Cockneys still say *gardin* for "garden", *year'oles* for "earholes" and *chimbley* for "chimney". There is a continuity in the pronunciation of *th*, which is often replaced by *f*, as in *barf* for "bath", or by *v*, as in *bruvver* for "brother" or *bovver* for "bother". The related loss to this is the "glottal stop", the neglect of the *t* in words like "butter", "bottle", "rotten" which in Cockney can best be represented as *bu!er, bo!le, ro!en*. Similarly, "didn't" becomes *didn* and "haven't" turns into *'avn*. The only alternative to the redundant *t* is *d*, as in *geddoud of i'*, or *you bedder no'*. The characteristic for which Cockney is famous, of course, is the silent *h*. Barltrop points out the dropped *h* has nothing to do with ignorance. He tells the story of the child reading a picture-book with its father. They turn the page and the father says: "That's an 'edgeog. It's really two words. Edge and og. They both start with an aitch."

Then there is a whole class of speech characteristics which betray the rural roots of Cockney. For instance, it is very common to find the *g* missing from *ing* endings like: *eatin'*, and *drinkin'*. This is precisely the speech of Fielding's Squire Western and his heirs in English literature. Even now it is fashionable, in certain parts of the English shires, to talk about *shootin'* or *fishin'*. Similarly, the Cockney pronunciation of "gone", "off" and "cough" *(gorn, orf,* and *corf)* is still used by upper-class country speakers without a trace of class-shame. The characteristic long *o*, *oo*, for *ew*, almost certainly originated in East Anglia: so it is no surprise that Cockneys and Americans have a number of pronunciations in common, including the *oo* for *ew*. Cockneys say *stoo* for "stew", *nood* for "nude", *noos* for "news", just like many Americans. In some respects, Cockney preserves in a vital form uses of English eradicated by education and the drive towards standardization.

Cockneys will drop letters and slur words in many different ways. "Old" becomes *ol'*. "An" becomes *ern,* as in *ern afternoon.* "You", as everyone who has attempted to render Cockney in print knows, is *yer.* The *o* in words like "tomato" and "potato" becomes *er,* as in *barrer* for "barrow". The main shopping street in Hackney, the Narrow Way, is known as the *Narraway.* Words get run together in Cockney. "God help us" becomes *gawdelpus,* and "God blind me" becomes *gorblimey.* Lesser examples like *lotta* for "lot of" pop up in unlikely places. A recent British Milk Marketing Board campaign played on Cockney slang and pronunciation—and an implicit toughness—with the copy-line *Gotta lotta bottle.*

One element of Cockney that has permeated the mainstream of the language is rhyming slang: a *bull and a cow* for "a row", and *Cain and Abel* for "a table". The popular view which holds that Cockney is, essentially, composed of this comes from the music-hall image of the Cockney—the cheeky chappy, with a heart of gold and a joke on his lips, who shows true grit in hard times and knows how to have a party when the day is over. In fact, until the 1930s, the currency of rhyming slang was quite small—Shaw, for instance, never used it. For many Cockneys, it was merely cheerful word play, in which a "suit" became a *whistle and flute,* a "hat" was a *titfer* or *tit-for-tat,* "gloves" were *turtles,* or *turtle-doves* and "boots" were *daisies* or *daisyroots.* . . .

Some famous examples of rhyming slang also have an undertone of comment—*trouble and strife* (wife), *holy friar* (liar), and *bees and honey* (money). *Rabbit*, which is short for *rabbit and pork* (talk), has now passed into the mainstream of English in the common phrase *rabbiting on*. When the entertainment industry took hold of rhyming slang, however, and put it in the mouths of Cockney characters like Alf Garnett and Arthur "Arfur" Daley, it became elevated into a kind of Cockney code. . . .

Another kind of slang that has largely escaped the pens of the scriptwriters is back slang:

> In the middle of the nineteenth century back slang was used as a secret language by street traders and costermongers. The people who use it now are mostly butchers and Thames lightermen. Instead of saying numbers like "one" and "two", you say "eno" and "rouf" and "evif" and "xis". Instead of saying "an old woman", you say "a delo namow". Instead of saying someone's fat, you say they're "taf" . . . "Yob" is the best known back slang word. It simply means "boy". "Yobbo" is a different thing. "Yobbo" is the Irishman's "boyo" backwards, and a "boyo" is a fellow who hangs about street corners, one of the lads, a larrikin.

Cockney survives, but the East End is not what it was. The Blitz flattened much of the area and dealt a body-blow to the London docks, a vital source of local livelihood. The urban planning of the 1960s and 1970s, in particular the creation of high-rise flats, accelerated the erosion of the old community and its traditions. But some aspects of the Cockney way of life die hard: the market at Spitalfields, which has a history running back to the days of Charles II, still does brisk business each morning. Market gardeners and greengrocers trade in fruit and vegetables in the early hours of the morning, as they have for generations. Artie Welsh is a salesman for Mays, the wholesalers.

> When you're serving two or three people at the same time you'll be allowing maybe two or three different prices out as well. I'll talk slang to the bloke who understands it. I'll be talking to someone. I'll say, "Right, George, you can be a rouf there." And he knows I've sold to him at four pounds, and the other person who's buying at five doesn't know.

The numbers have their equivalent in slang. *Nicker* is "one", *bottle* is "two", *carpet* is "three", *rouf* is "four", *jacks* is "five", *Tom Nicks* is "six", *neves* is "seven", *garden gate* is "eight", "ten" is *cock-and-hen*, or *cockle*. . . .

Cockney is as magpie-minded as Standard English. It has borrowed widely: from the Empire, from the gypsies, from the English Jews, from the two World Wars, and, indeed, from any outsider who came up with a word that caught the popular fancy. For instance, *skive*, widely attributed to the Cockneys, a now well-established word for "shirk" or "play truant", is a local Lincolnshire word.

From the armies of the British Empire, stationed in India and the Far East, Cockney picked up words like *buckshee*, the Cockney word for "free", strictly speaking "surplus", or "going a-begging". *Doolally*, from Deolali (a town near Bombay and site of a mental hospital for British troops), is "demented", "barmy". "Let's have a *"shufti"*, a Hindustani word, means "let's have a look around". One piece of rhyming slang, *khyber* for "backside", came from the British soldiers stationed on the Khyber Pass.

Romany became part of Cockney in the nineteenth century as the population of East London grew. Gypsy traders—known as *pikeys*—brought their stalls and set up street markets, creating what one writer called a perpetual fair in Whitechapel Road. From the gypsies, Cockney derives words like *mush* (mouth or face), as in *Oi, mush,* meaning, "Here, mate". This Romany derivation is found in the mouths of the gypsies in the novels of George Borrow (*Romany Rye,* for instance). *Pucker,* meaning "to talk", is also Romany, so is *chavvy,* "a child". Romany lingo survives in Cockney talk to this day. As Bob Barltrop says:

> A word that everybody knows is "pal" for friend. This is actually the Romany word for brother. "Dukes" is for hands, and this is the Cockney's favourite word for them, as in "Give us your dukes, mate." Romany palm-reading is called "dukering".

Many Cockney expressions have Yiddish roots. The Jewish community in the East End flourished throughout the last century and reached its cultural peak in the years before the First World War. Cockney trader and Jewish manufacturer have worked alongside for generations. *Shemozzle,* a favourite Cockney word for "confusion", is obviously Jewish. So is *stumer* for "a dead loss", *schmutter* for "clothing" and *schlemiel* for "an idiot". *Clobber* (clothes) has Yiddish roots; so does *gelt* for "money", and *nosh* for "food". *Gezumph* meaning to swindle has now passed into the lexicon as *gazump,* familiar in estate agencies throughout the land. *Spiel* originates, in Britain, in the East End; so does *donah* for woman. Both have obvious Yiddish roots. All Cockneys know—and still use—*mazel tov* for "good luck".

Finally, the World Wars added their store of words (mainly French) to the Cockney vocabulary. A *parlyvoo* (from *parlez-vous*) still means "a talking session". *San fairy ann* for "it doesn't matter" (from *ça ne fait rien*) is still common. So is *ally toot sweet* (from *allez tout de suite* i.e. "hurry up"). . . .

Part of the Cockney fascination with all kinds of languages comes from what Bob Barltrop calls their love of "grand sounding words to which they can attach a special meaning, words which you can say really majestically". Barltrop has three favourite examples:

> "Diabolical"—and not just "a diabolical liberty". If you can say with presence, "that's absolutely dia-bol-ical, innit", that sounds great. Another word of which Cockneys are immensely fond is "impunity", as in "He walks in and out of 'ere with impunity." Yet another is "chronic". "Chronic" is associated with a long illness, something that goes on for a long time and is terribly painful. So if you ask your friend what the film was like and he didn't enjoy it, he will say, "Gorblimey, it was chronic."

The distinctive greetings of Cockney include *'Ow're yer goin'* meaning "How are you doing?" "How's things?" "What's new?" Of all the identifying words attached to such questions—from *mate* to *guvnor*, to *chum, dear, love* and *duck,* the most important is probably *mate,* associated with Cockney and Australian English throughout the world. *Mate* covers all relationships that are important, after the family ones (but including wives). A "mate" is more than a friend: it suggests a mutuality and closeness beyond mere friendship. After mate, there are *the mates*, the people you mix with socially.

For all the Londoners and other city folk, Irish immigrants, landless labourers, debtors, hustlers and swindlers who headed for the colonies throughout the nineteenth century, the idea of friendship in adversity, of mates, of pals, even of chums, was fundamental to the experience of exile. New South Wales, New Zealand, and the Cape colony: these were all harsh, unfamiliar environments. And not since the Anglo-Saxons landed in Britain, or the Elizabethans in North America, was there such a need or such an opportunity for word and phrase-making.

Mother Tongue

by Amy Tan

Should all residents of an English-speaking country speak a standard form of English? In the following essay, a prominent Asian-American writer discusses not only the limitations that are often associated with people who speak "broken" English, but also the intimacy that results from their special language.

I am not a scholar of English or literature. I cannot give you much more than personal opinions on the English language and its variations in this country or others.

I am a writer. And by that definition, I am someone who has always loved language. I am fascinated by language in daily life. I spend a great deal of my time thinking about the power of language—the way it can evoke an emotion, a visual image, a complex idea, or a simple truth. Language is the tool of my trade. And I use them all—all the Englishes I grew up with.

Recently, I was made keenly aware of the different Englishes I do use. I was giving a talk to a large group of people, the same talk I had already given to half a dozen other groups. The nature of the talk was about my writing, my life, and my book, *The Joy Luck Club*. The talk was going along well enough, until I remembered one major difference that made the whole talk sound wrong. My mother was in the room. And it was perhaps the first time she had heard me give a lengthy speech, using the kind of English I have never used with her. I was saying things like, "The intersection of memory upon imagination" and

"There is an aspect of my fiction that relates to thus-and-thus"—a speech filled with carefully wrought grammatical phrases, burdened, it suddenly seemed to me, with nominalized forms, past perfect tenses, conditional phrases, all the forms of standard English that I had learned in school and through books, the forms of English I did not use at home with my mother.

Just last week, I was walking down the street with my mother, and I again found myself conscious of the English I was using, the English I do use with her. We were talking about the price of new and used furniture and I heard myself saying this: "Not waste money that way." My husband was with us as well, and he didn't notice any switch in my English. And then I realized why. It's because over the twenty years we've been together I've often used that same kind of English with him, and sometimes he even uses it with me. It has become our language of intimacy, a different sort of English that relates to family talk, the language I grew up with.

So you'll have some idea of what this family talk I heard sounds like, I'll quote what my mother said during a recent conversation which I videotaped and then transcribed. During this conversation, my mother was talking about a political gangster in Shanghai who had the same last name as her family's, Du, and how the gangster in his early years wanted to be adopted by her family, which was rich by comparison. Later, the gangster became more powerful, far richer than my mother's family, and one day showed up at my mother's wedding to pay his respects. Here's what she said in part:

"Du Yusong having business like fruit stand. Like off the street kind. He is Du like Du Zong—but not Tsung-ming Island people. The local people call putong, the river east side, he belong to that side local people. That man want to ask Du Zong father take him in like become own family. Du Zong father wasn't look down on him, but didn't take seriously, until that man big like become a mafia. Now important person, very hard to inviting him. Chinese way, came only to show respect, don't stay for dinner. Respect for making big celebration, he shows up. Mean gives lots of respect. Chinese custom. Chinese social life that way. If too important won't have to stay too long. He come to my wedding. I didn't see, I heard it. I gone to boy's side, they have YMCA dinner. Chinese age I was nineteen."

You should know that my mother's expressive command of English belies how much she actually understands. She reads the *Forbes* report, listens to *Wall Street Week,* converses daily with her stockbroker, reads all of Shirley MacLaine's books with ease—all kinds of things I can't begin to understand. Yet some of my friends tell me they understand 50 percent of what my mother says. Some say they understand 80 to 90 percent. Some say they understand none of it, as if she were speaking pure Chinese. But to me, my mother's English is perfectly clear, perfectly natural. It's my mother tongue. Her language, as I hear it, is vivid, direct, full of observation and imagery. That was the language that helped shape the way I saw things, expressed things, made sense of the world.

Lately, I've been giving more thought to the kind of English my mother speaks. Like others, I have described it to people as "broken" or "fractured" English. But I wince when I say that. It has always bothered me that I can think of no way to describe it other than "broken," as if it were damaged and needed to be fixed, as if it lacked a certain wholeness and soundness. I've heard other terms used, "limited

English," for example. But they seem just as bad, as if everything is limited, including people's perceptions of the limited English speaker.

I know this for a fact, because when I was growing up, my mother's "limited" English limited *my* perception of her. I was ashamed of her English. I believed that her English reflected the quality of what she had to say. That is, because she expressed them imperfectly her thoughts were imperfect. And I had plenty of empirical evidence to support me: the fact that people in department stores, at banks, and at restaurants did not take her seriously, did not give her good service, pretended not to understand her, or even acted as if they did not hear her.

My mother has long realized the limitations of her English as well. When I was fifteen, she used to have me call people on the phone to pretend I was she. In this guise, I was forced to ask for information or even to complain and yell at people who had been rude to her. One time it was a call to her stockbroker in New York. She had cashed out her small portfolio and it just so happened we were going to go to New York the next week, our very first trip outside California. I had to get on the phone and say in an adolescent voice that was not very convincing, "This is Mrs. Tan."

And my mother was standing in the back whispering loudly, "Why he don't send me check, already two weeks late. So mad he lie to me, losing me money."

And then I said in perfect English, "Yes, I'm getting rather concerned. You had agreed to send the check two weeks ago, but it hasn't arrived."

Then she began to talk more loudly. "What he want, I come to New York tell him front of his boss, you cheating me?" And I was trying to calm her down, make her be quiet, while telling the stockbroker, "I can't tolerate any more excuses. If I don't receive the check immediately, I am going to have to speak to your manager when I'm in New York next week." And sure enough, the following week there we were in front of this astonished stockbroker, and I was sitting there red-faced and quiet, and my mother, the real Mrs. Tan, was shouting at his boss in her impeccable broken English.

We used a similar routine just five days ago, for a situation that was far less humorous. My mother had gone to the hospital for an appointment, to find out about a benign brain tumor a CAT scan had revealed a month ago. She said she had spoken very good English, her best English, no mistakes. Still, she said, the hospital did not apologize when they said they had lost the CAT scan and she had come for nothing. She said they did not seem to have any sympathy when she told them she was anxious to know the exact diagnosis, since her husband and son had both died of brain tumors. She said they would not give her any more information until the next time and she would have to make another appointment for that. So she said she would not leave until the doctor called her daughter. She wouldn't budge. And when the doctor finally called her daughter, me, who spoke in perfect English—lo and behold—we had assurances the CAT scan would be found, promises that a conference call on Monday would be held, and apologies for any suffering my mother had gone through for a most regrettable mistake.

I think my mother's English almost had an effect on limiting my possibilities in life as well. Sociologists and linguists probably will tell you that a person's developing language skills are more influenced by peers. But I do think that the language spoken in the family, especially in immigrant families which are more insular, plays a large role in shaping the language of the child. And I believe that it affected my results on achievement tests, IQ tests, and the SAT. While my English skills were never judged as poor, compared to math, English could not be considered my strong suit. In grade school I did moderately well, getting perhaps B's, sometimes B-pluses, in English and scoring perhaps in the sixtieth or seventieth percentile on achievement tests. But those scores were not good enough to override the opinion that my true abilities lay in math and science, because in those areas I achieved A's and scored in the ninetieth percentile or higher.

This was understandable. Math is precise; there is only one correct answer. Whereas, for me at least, the answers on English tests were always a judgment call, a matter of opinion and personal experience. Those tests were constructed around items like fill-in-the-blank sentence completion, such as, "Even though Tom was _____, Mary thought he was _____." And the correct answer always seemed to be the most bland combinations of thoughts, for example, "Even though Tom was shy, Mary thought he was charming," with the grammatical structure "even though" limiting the correct answer to some sort of semantic opposites, so you wouldn't get answers like, "Even though Tom was foolish, Mary thought he was ridiculous." Well, according to my mother, there were very few limitations as to what Tom could have been and what Mary might have thought of him. So I never did well on tests like that.

The same was true with word analogies, pairs of words in which you were supposed to find some sort of logical, semantic relationship—for example, "*Sunset* is to *nightfall* as _____ is to _____." And here you would be presented with a list of four possible pairs, one of which showed the same kind of relationship: *red* is to *stoplight, bus* is to *arrival, chills* is to *fever, yawn* is to *boring*. Well, I could never think that way. I knew what the tests were asking, but I could not block out of my mind the images already created by the first pair, *"sunset* is to *nightfall"*—and I would see a burst of colors against a darkening sky, the moon rising, the lowering of a curtain of stars. And all the other pairs of words—red, bus, stoplight, boring—just threw up a mass of confusing images, making it impossible for me to sort out something as logical as saying: "A sunset precedes nightfall" is the same as "a chill precedes a fever." The only way I would have gotten that answer right would have been to imagine an associative situation, for example, my being disobedient and staying out past sunset, catching a chill at night, which turns into feverish pneumonia as punishment, which indeed did happen to me.

I have been thinking about all this lately, about my mother's English, about achievement tests. Because lately I've been asked, as a writer, why there are not more Asian Americans represented in American literature. Why are there few Asian Americans enrolled in creative writing programs? Why do so many Chinese students go into engineering? Well, these are broad sociological questions I can't begin to answer. But I have noticed in surveys—in fact, just last week—that Asian students, as a whole, always do significantly better on math achievement tests than in English. And this makes me think that there are other Asian-American students whose English spoken in the home might also be described as "broken" or "limited." And perhaps they also have teachers who are steering them away from writing and into math and science, which is what happened to me.

Fortunately, I happen to be rebellious in nature and enjoy the challenge of disproving assumptions made about me. I became an English major my first year in college, after being enrolled as pre-med. I started writing nonfiction as a freelancer the week after I was told by my former boss that writing was my worst skill and I should hone my talents toward account management.

But it wasn't until 1985 that I finally began to write fiction. And at first I wrote using what I thought to be wittily crafted sentences, sentences that would finally prove I had mastery over the English language. Here's an example from the first draft of a story that later made its way into The Joy Luck Club, but without this line: "That was my mental quandary in its nascent state." A terrible line, which I can barely pronounce.

Fortunately, for reasons I won't get into today, I later decided I should envision a reader for the stories I would write. And the reader I decided upon was my mother, because these were stories about mothers. So with this reader in mind—and in fact she did read my early drafts—I began to write stories using all the Englishes I grew up with: the English I spoke to my mother, which for lack of a better term might be described as "simple"; the English she used with me, which for lack of a better term might be described as "broken"; my translation of her Chinese, which could certainly be described as "watered down"; and what I imagined to be her translation of her Chinese if she could speak in perfect English, her internal language, and for that I sought to preserve the essence, but neither an English nor a Chinese structure. I wanted to capture what language ability tests can never reveal: her intent, her passion, her imagery, the rhythms of her speech and the nature of her thoughts.

Apart from what any critic had to say about my writing, I knew I had succeeded where it counted when my mother finished reading my book and gave me her verdict: "So easy to read."

Two Words

by Isabel Allende
translated by Alberto Manguel

*"Words are cheap," or so the saying goes.
Yet Eliza Doolittle is willing to spend all
her money to learn how to pronounce
them properly. The following story shows
another young woman who uses language
to lift herself out of poverty.*

Her name was Belisa Crepusculario, not through
baptism or because of her mother's insight, but because
she herself sought it out until she found it, and dressed
herself in it. Her occupation consisted of selling words.
She travelled through the country, from the highest and
coldest regions to the scorching coast, setting up in
markets and fairs four sticks with a cloth awning, under
which she protected herself from the sun and the rain to
see to her customers. She had no need to call out her
wares, because with so much walking here and there
everybody knew her. There were those who waited for
her year in, year out, and when she appeared in the
village with her bundle under her arm they would line
up in front of her stall. Her prices were fair. For five
cents she would give out poems learnt by heart; for
seven she would improve the quality of dreams; for nine
she would write love letters; for twelve she would make
up insults for irreconcilable enemies. She also sold
stories; not fantastical tales but long, true chronicles
which she would recite from beginning to end, without
skipping a word. That is how she would carry the news
from one village to the next. People would pay her to
add one or two lines: a child was born, so-and-so died,
our children were married, the harvest caught fire. In

each place people would sit around her to listen to her when she began to speak, and that is how they would learn about the lives of others, of faraway relatives, the ins and outs of the civil war. To anyone who bought fifty cents' worth she'd give as a gift a secret word to frighten melancholy away. Of course, it wasn't the same word for all—that would have been collective deception. Each one received his own, certain that no one, in the entire universe and beyond, would use that word to that specific end.

Belisa Crepuscularo was born into a poor family, so poor that they did not even have names to call their children. She came into the world and grew up in the most inhospitable of regions and until her twelfth birthday she had no other virtue or occupation than surviving the hunger and thirst of centuries. During an interminable drought she was forced to bury four younger brothers, and when she understood that her turn had come she decided to set forth across the plains towards the sea, wondering whether on the road she might be able to trick death. She was so stubborn that she succeeded, and not only did she save her own life but also, by chance, she discovered the art of writing. As she reached a village near the coast, the wind dropped at her feet a newspaper page. She lifted the yellow and brittle piece of paper and stood there a long while staring at it, unable to guess its use, until her curiosity overcame her shyness. She approached a man washing his horse in the same muddy waters where she had quenched her thirst.

'What is this?' she asked.

'The sports page of a newspaper,' the man answered, not at all surprised at her ignorance.

The answer left the girl astonished, but she didn't want to seem impudent, so she simply inquired about the meaning of the tiny fly legs drawn on the paper.

'They are words, child. Here it says that Fulgencio

Barba knocked out Tiznao the Black in the third round.'

That day Belisa Crepusculario found out that words fly about loose, with no master, and that anyone with a little cunning can catch them and start a trade. She reflected on her own situation, and realized that, other than becoming a prostitute or a servant in a rich man's kitchen, there were few jobs that she could do. Selling words seemed to her a decent alternative. From that moment she worked at that profession and never took on another. At first she offered her wares without suspecting that words could be written in other places than newspapers. When she became aware of this, she worked out the infinite projections of her business, paid a priest twenty pesos to teach her to read and write, and with the three pesos left over from her savings bought herself a dictionary. She perused it from A to Z, and then threw it into the sea, because she had no intention of swindling her clients with prepackaged words.

One August morning Belisa Crepusculario was sitting under her awning, selling words of justice to an old man who for twenty years had been requesting his pension, when a group of horsemen burst into the marketplace. They were the Colonel's men led by the Mulatto who was known throughout the area for the quickness of his knife and his loyalty towards his chief. Both men, the Colonel and the Mulatto, had spent their lives busy with the civil war, and their names were irremediably linked to calamity and plunder. The warriors arrived in a cloak of noise and dust and as they advanced the terror of a hurricane spread across the marketplace. The chickens escaped in a flutter, the dogs bolted, the women ran away with their children, and there was not a single soul left in the marketplace, except Belisa Crepusculario, who had never before seen the Mulatto, and who was therefore surprised when he addressed her.

'It is you I'm after,' he shouted, pointing at her with his rolled-up whip, and even before he finished saying so two men fell upon Belisa Crepuscolario, trampling her tent and breaking her inkwell, tied her hands and feet, and laid her like a sailor's sack across the rump of the mulatto's mount. They set off southwards at a gallop.

Hours later, when Belisa Crepuscolario felt she was on the point of dying with her heart turned to sand by the shaking of the horse, she realized that they were stopping and that four powerful hands were placing her on the ground. She tried to stand up and raise her head with dignity, but her strength failed her and she collapsed with a sigh, sinking into a dazzling sleep. She awoke several hours afterwards to the murmur of night, but she had no time to decipher the sounds because as she opened her eyes she was met by the impatient eyes of the Mulatto, kneeling by her side.

'You're awake at last, woman,' he said, offering his canteen for her to drink a sip of firewater mixed with gunpowder to jolt her back to life.

She wanted to know why she had been so mistreated, and he explained that the Colonel required her services. He allowed her to wet her face, and immediately led her to the far end of the camp where the man most feared in the entire land lay resting in a hammock suspended between two trees. She couldn't see his face because it lay hidden in the uncertain shade of the foliage and the ineffaceable shadow of many years living as an outlaw, but she imagined that it must be terrible if the Mulatto addressed him in such humble tones. She was taken aback by his voice, soft and mellifluous like that of a scholar.

'Are you the one who sells words?'

'At your service,' she mumbled, screwing up her eyes to see him better in the gloom.

The Colonel rose to his feet and the light in the

Mulatto's torch hit him full in the face. She saw his dark skin and his fierce puma eyes, and realized at once that she was facing the loneliest man in the world.

'I want to be president,' he said. He was tired of roaming this cursed land fighting tireless wars and suffering defeats that no trick could turn into victories. For many years now he had slept in the open, bitten by mosquitoes, feeding on iguanas and rattlesnake soup, but these minor inconveniences were not reason enough to change his fate. What really bothered him was the terror in other men's eyes. He wanted to enter villages under arcs of triumph, among coloured banners and flowers, with crowds cheering him and bringing him gifts of fresh eggs and freshly baked bread. He was fed up with seeing how men fled from his approach, how women aborted in fright, and children trembled. Because of this, he wanted to become president. The Mulatto had suggested they ride to the capital and gallop into the palace to take over the government, in the same way that they took so many other things without asking anyone's permission. But the Colonel had no wish to become simply another dictator, because there had been quite enough of those and anyhow that was no way for him to coax affection from the people. His idea was to be chosen by popular vote in the December elections.

'For that, I need to speak like a candidate. Can you sell me the words for a speech?' the Colonel asked Belisa Crepusculario.

She had accepted many different requests, but none like this one, and yet she felt she could not refuse, for fear that the Mulatto would shoot her between the eyes or, even worse, that the Colonel would burst into tears. Also, she felt an urge to help him, because she became aware of a tingling heat on her skin, a powerful desire to touch this man, go over him with her hands, hold him in her arms.

All night long and much of the following day Belisa Crepusculario rummaged through her stock for words that would suit a presidential oration, while the Mulatto kept a close watch on her, unable to tear his eyes away from her strong walker's legs and untouched breasts. She cast aside words that were dry and harsh, words that were too flowery, too faded through too much use, words that made improbable promises, words lacking truth, muddled words, and was left with only those words that were able to reach unerringly men's thoughts and women's intuitions. Making use of the skills bought from the priest for twenty pesos, she wrote out the speech on a sheet of paper and signalled at the Mulatto for him to untie the rope that held her by the ankles to a tree. She was brought once more into the Colonel's presence, and seeing him again, again she felt the same tingling anxiety she had felt at their first meeting. She gave him the sheet of paper and waited, while he stared at it, holding it with only the tips of his fingers.

'What in Hell's name does it say here?' he asked at last.

'Can't you read?'

'What I know is how to make war,' he answered.

She read him the speech out loud. She read it three times, so that he would be able to learn it by heart. When she finished, she saw the emotion drawn on the faces of his soldiers who had assembled to listen to her, and noticed that the Colonel's yellow eyes were shining with excitement, certain that with these words the presidential seat would be his.

'If after hearing it three times, the boys still have their mouths open, then this stuff works, my Colonel,' approved the Mulatto.

'How much do I owe you for your job, woman?' the chief asked.

'One peso, my Colonel.'

'That's not expensive,' he said, opening the pouch which hung from his belt with the leftovers from the latest booty.

'And you also have a right to a bonus. You can have two secret words, for free,' said Belisa Crepuscolario.

'How's that?'

She explained to him that for every fifty cents a customer spent, she gave away one word for his exclusive use. The chief shrugged, because he had no interest in her offer, but he didn't want to seem impolite with one who had served him so well. Slowly she approached the leather stool on which he was sitting, and leaned over to give him his two words. Then the man caught a whiff of the mountain smell on her skin, the fiery heat of her hips, the terrible brushing of her hair against him, the wild mint breath whispering into his ear the two secret words that were his by right.

'They're yours, my Colonel,' she said, drawing back. 'You may use them as much as you wish.'

The Mulatto escorted Belisa to the edge of the road, never taking his begging mongrel eyes off her, but when he stretched out his hand to touch her she stopped him with a gush of made-up words that dampened his desire, because he believed they were some sort of irrevocable curse.

During the months of September, October, and November the Colonel delivered his speech so many times that, had it not been composed out of long-lasting and glittering words, the constant use would have turned the speech to ashes. He travelled across the country in all directions, riding into cities with a triumphant air, but stopping also in forgotten hamlets where only traces of garbage signalled a human presence, in order to convince the citizens to vote for him. While he spoke, standing on a platform in the middle of the marketplace, the Mulatto and his men distributed sweets and painted his name with scarlet frost on the walls. After the speech was over, the troops would light firecrackers, and when at last they rode away, a trail of hope remained for many days in midair, like the memory of a comet. Very soon the Colonel became the most popular candidate. It was something never seen before—this man sprung from the civil war, crisscrossed with scars and speaking like a scholar, whose renown spread across the nation moving the very heart of the country. The press began to take notice. Journalists travelled from afar to interview him and repeat his words, and the number of his followers grew, as well as the number of his enemies.

'We're doing fine, my Colonel,' said the Mulatto after twelve weeks of success.

But the candidate did not hear him. He was repeating his two secret words, as he now did more and more frequently. He would repeat them when nostalgia made him soft, he would murmur them in his sleep, he would carry them with him on horseback, he would think of them just before pronouncing his celebrated speech, and he would surprise himself savouring them at careless moments. And every time these two words sprang to his mind, he would scent the mountain perfume, the fiery heat, the terrible brushing, and the wild mint breath, until he began to roam around like a sleep-walker, and his very own men realized that his life would come to an end before he reached the presidential seat.

'What's happening to you, my Colonel?' the Mulatto asked many times, until one day the chief could bear it no longer and confessed that the two words he carried embedded in his gut were to blame for his mood.

'Tell them to me, to see if that way they lose their power,' his faithful assistant begged him.

'I won't, they belong to me alone,' the Colonel answered.

Tired of seeing his chief weaken like a man condemned to death, the Mulatto slung his rifle over his shoulder and set off in search of Belisa Crepusculario. He followed her traces throughout the vastness of the land, until he found her under her awning, telling her rosary of tales. He stood in front of her, legs spread out and weapon in hand.

'You're coming with me,' he ordered.

She was waiting for him. She picked up her inkwell, folded her awning, draped her shawl over her shoulders, and without saying a word climbed onto the back of his horse. During the whole journey they never even motioned to one another, because the Mulatto's lust for her had turned to anger and only the fear of her tongue stopped him from whipping her to shreds, as he would have done with anyone else in a similar situation; nor was he willing to tell her how the Colonel went about in a daze, and how what had not been achieved by so many years of battling had suddenly been wrought by a charm whispered in his ear. Two days later they reached the camp and he immediately took the prisoner to the candidate, in front of all the troops.

'I've brought you this witch so that you can give her back her words, my Colonel, and she can give you back your manhood,' he said, pointing the rifle's muzzle at the woman's neck.

The Colonel and Belisa Crepusculari gazed at one another for a long moment, measuring one another at a distance. The men then understood that their chief would never be able to rid himself of the charm of those two cursed words, because as they looked on, they saw how the bloodthirsty eyes of the puma softened as the woman now stepped forward and held him by the hand.

The Model

by Bernard Malamud

*When Pickering asks Higgins whether he
thinks Eliza has any feelings, Higgins
replies, "Not any feelings that we need
bother about." He eventually learns that
he has underestimated both Eliza's and his
own emotional involvement in the
experiment. The following story is about a
painter who hires a young woman to pose
for him. Does he make the same mistake
as Higgins?*

Early one morning Ephraim Elihu rang up the Art
Students League and asked them how he could locate
an experienced female model he could paint nude. He
told the woman speaking to him on the phone that he
wanted someone of about thirty. "Could you possibly
help me?"

"I don't recognize your name," said the woman on
the telephone. "Have you ever dealt with us before?
Some of our students will work as models but usually
only for painters we know." Mr. Elihu said he hadn't.
He wanted it understood he was an amateur painter
who had once studied at the League.

"Do you have a studio?"

"It's a large living room with lots of light.

"I'm no youngster," he went on, "but after many
years I've begun painting again and I'd like to do some
nude studies to get back my feeling for form. I'm not
a professional painter you understand but I'm serious
about painting. If you want any references as to my
character, I can supply them." He asked her what the
going rate for models was, and the woman, after a
pause, said, "Six-fifty the hour." Mr. Elihu said that

was satisfactory. He seemed to want to talk longer but she did not encourage him. She wrote down his name and address and said she thought she could have someone for him the day after tomorrow. He thanked her for her consideration.

That was on Wednesday. The model appeared on Friday morning. She had telephoned the night before and they settled on a time for her to come. She rang his bell shortly after 9 a.m. and Mr. Elihu went at once to the door. He was a gray-haired man of seventy who lived in a brownstone house near Ninth Avenue, and he was excited by the prospect of painting this young woman.

The model was a plain-looking woman of twenty-seven or so, and the old painter decided her best feature was her eyes. She was wearing a blue raincoat on a clear spring day. The old painter liked her face but kept that to himself. She barely glanced at him as she walked firmly into the room.

"Good day," he said, and she answered, "Good day."

"It's like spring," said the old man. "The foliage is starting up again."

"Where do you want me to change?" asked the model.

Mr. Elihu asked her name and she responded, "Ms. Perry."

"You can change in the bathroom, I would say, Miss Perry, or if you like, my own room—down the hall—is empty and you can change there also. It's warmer than the bathroom."

The model said it made no difference to her but she thought she would rather change in the bathroom.

"That is as you wish," said the elderly man.

"Is your wife around?" she then asked, glancing into the room.

"I happen to be a widower."

He said he had had a daughter once but she had died in an accident.

The model said she was sorry. "I'll change and be out in a few fast minutes."

"No hurry at all," said Mr. Elihu, glad he was about to paint her.

Ms. Perry entered the bathroom, undressed there, and returned quickly. She slipped off her terry cloth robe. Her head and shoulders were slender and well formed. She asked the old man how he would like her to pose. He was standing by an enamel-top kitchen table in a living room with a large window. On the tabletop he had squeezed out, and was mixing together, the contents of two small tubes of paint. There were three other tubes he did not touch. The model, taking a last drag of a cigarette, pressed it out against a coffee can lid on the kitchen table.

"I hope you don't mind if I take a puff once in a while?"

"I don't mind, if you do it when we take a break."

"That's all I meant."

She was watching him as he slowly mixed his colors.

Mr. Elihu did not immediately look at her nude body but said he would like her to sit in the chair by the window. They were facing a back yard with an ailanthus tree whose leaves had just come out.

"How would you like me to sit, legs crossed or not crossed?"

"However you prefer that. Crossed or uncrossed doesn't make much of a difference to me. Whatever makes you feel comfortable."

The model seemed surprised at that, but she sat down in the yellow chair by the window and crossed one leg over the other. Her figure was good.

"Is this O.K. for you?"

Mr. Elihu nodded. "Fine," he said. "Very fine."

He dipped the brush into the paint he had mixed on the tabletop, and after glancing at the model's nude body, began to paint. He would look at her, then look quickly away, as if he was afraid of affronting her. But his expression was objective. He painted apparently casually, from time to time gazing up at the model. He did not often look at her. She seemed not to be aware of him. Once, she turned to observe the ailanthus tree and he studied her momentarily to see what she might have seen in it.

Then she began to watch the painter with interest. She watched his eyes and she watched his hands. He wondered if he was doing something wrong. At the end of about an hour she rose impatiently from the yellow chair.

"Tired?" he asked.

"It isn't that," she said, "but I would like to know what in the name of Christ you think you are doing? I frankly don't think you know the first thing about painting."

She had astonished him. He quickly covered the canvas with a towel.

After a long moment, Mr. Elihu, breathing shallowly, wet his dry lips and said he was making no claims for himself as a painter. He said he had tried to make that absolutely clear to the woman he had talked to at the art school when he had called.

Then he said, "I might have made a mistake in asking you to come to this house today. I think I should have tested myself a while longer, just so I wouldn't be wasting anybody's time. I guess I am not ready to do what I would like to do."

"I don't care how long you have tested yourself," said Ms. Perry. "I honestly don't think you have painted me at all. In fact, I felt you weren't interested in painting me. I think you're interested in letting your eyes go over my naked body for certain reasons of your own. I don't know what your personal needs are but I'm damn well sure that most of them are not about painting."

"I guess I have made a mistake."

"I guess you have," said the model. She had her robe on now, the belt pulled tight.

"I'm a painter," she said, "and I model because I am broke but I know a fake when I see one."

"I wouldn't feel so bad," said Mr. Elihu, "if I hadn't gone out of my way to explain the situation to that lady at the Art Students League.

"I'm sorry this happened," Mr. Elihu said hoarsely. "I should have thought it through but didn't. I'm seventy years of age. I have always loved women and felt a sad loss that I have no particular women friends at this time of my life. That's one of the reasons I wanted to paint again, though I make no claims that I was ever greatly talented. Also, I guess I didn't realize how much about painting I have forgotten. Not only that, but about the female body. I didn't realize I would be so moved by yours, and, on reflection, about the way my life has gone. I hoped painting again would refresh my feeling for life. I regret that I have inconvenienced and disturbed you."

"I'll be paid for my inconvenience," Ms. Perry said, "but what you can't pay me for is the insult of coming here and submitting myself to your eyes crawling on my body."

"I didn't mean it as an insult."

"That's what it feels like to me."

She then asked Mr. Elihu to disrobe.

"I?" he said, surprised. "What for?"

"I want to sketch you. Take your pants and shirt off."

He said he had barely got rid of his winter underwear but she did not smile.

Mr. Elihu disrobed, ashamed of how he must look to her.

With quick strokes she sketched his form. He was not a bad-looking man but felt bad. When she had the sketch she dipped his brush into a blob of black pigment she had squeezed out of a tube and smeared his features, leaving a black mess.

He watched her hating him but said nothing.

Ms. Perry tossed the brush into a wastebasket and returned to the bathroom for her clothing.

The old man wrote out a check for her for the sum they had agreed on. He was ashamed to sign his name but he signed it and handed it to her. Ms. Perry slipped the check into her large purse and left.

He thought that in her way she was not a bad-looking woman though she lacked grace. The old man then asked himself, "Is there nothing more to my life than it is now? Is this all that is left to me?"

The answer seemed yes and he wept at how old he had so quickly become.

Afterwards he removed the towel over his canvas and tried to fill in her face, but he had already forgotten it.

Words

by Vern Rutsala

*Professor Higgins believes that the first
step in reforming people is to teach them
to speak "proper" English. Is there nothing
worthwhile in the Cockney dialect? The
speaker in the following poem suggests
that bad grammar and impoverished
vocabulary might be a reflection of
awareness rather than ignorance.*

We had more than
we could use.
They embarrassed us,
our talk fuller than our
5   rooms. They named
nothing we could see—
*dining room, study,
mantel piece, lobster
thermidor.* They named
10   things you only
saw in movies—
the thin flicker Friday
nights that made us
feel empty in the cold
15   as we walked home
through our only great
abundance, snow.
This is why we said 'ain't'
and 'he don't'.
20   We wanted words to fit
our cold linoleum,
our oil lamps, our

outhouse. We knew
better but it was wrong
25   to use a language
that named ghosts,
nothing you could touch.
We left such words at school
locked in books
30   where they belonged.
It was the vocabulary
of our lives that was
so thin. We knew this
and grew to hate
35   all the words that named
the vacancy of our rooms—
looking here we said
studio couch and saw cot;
looking there we said
40   *venetian blinds* and saw only the yard;
brick meant tarpaper,
fireplace meant wood stove.
And this is why we came to love
the double negative.

Acknowledgments

(continued from page ii)

Simon & Schuster: "Two Words" from *The Stories of Eva Luna* by Isabel Allende, translated from Spanish by Margaret Sayers Peden; Copyright © 1989 by Isabel Allende, English translation Copyright © 1991 by Macmillan Publishing Company. Reprinted with the permission of Scribner, a Division of Simon & Schuster.

Farrar, Straus & Giroux, Inc.: "The Model" from *The Stories of Bernard Malamud* by Bernard Malamud; Copyright © 1983 by Bernard Malamud. Reprinted by permission of Farrar, Straus & Giroux, Inc.

Story Line Press: "Words" from *Selected Poems* by Vern Rutsala; Copyright © 1991 by Vern Rutsala. Reprinted by permission of Story Line Press, Three Oaks Farm, Brownsville, Oregon.